TECHNOLOGY ROADMAP
CASES AND OPPORTUNITIES

Editora Appris Ltda.
1.ª Edição - Copyright© 2024 dos autores
Direitos de Edição Reservados à Editora Appris Ltda.

Nenhuma parte desta obra poderá ser utilizada indevidamente, sem estar de acordo com a Lei nº 9.610/98. Se incorreções forem encontradas, serão de exclusiva responsabilidade de seus organizadores. Foi realizado o Depósito Legal na Fundação Biblioteca Nacional, de acordo com as Leis nᵒˢ 10.994, de 14/12/2004, e 12.192, de 14/01/2010.

Catalogação na Fonte
Elaborado por: Dayanne Leal Souza
Bibliotecária CRB 9/2162

B738t 2024	Borschiver, Suzana Technology roadmap: cases and opportunities / Suzana Borschiver e Aline Souza Tavares. – 1. ed. – Curitiba: Appris, 2024. 137 p. : il. color. ; 21 cm. (Geral). Inclui referências. ISBN 978-65-250-6260-0 1. Technology roadmap. 2. Innovation management. 3. Technology management. I. Borschiver, Suzana. II. Tavares, Aline Souza. III. Título. IV. Série. CDD - 600

Livro de acordo com a normalização técnica da ABNT

Appris editora

Editora e Livraria Appris Ltda.
Av. Manoel Ribas, 2265 – Mercês
Curitiba/PR – CEP: 80810-002
Tel. (41) 3156 - 4731
www.editoraappris.com.br

Printed in Brazil
Impresso no Brasil

Suzana Borschiver
Aline Souza Tavares

TECHNOLOGY ROADMAP

CASES AND OPPORTUNITIES

Appris
editora

Curitiba, PR
2024

FICHA TÉCNICA

EDITORIAL	Augusto Coelho
	Sara C. de Andrade Coelho
COMITÊ EDITORIAL	Ana El Achkar (UNIVERSO/RJ)
	Andréa Barbosa Gouveia (UFPR)
	Conrado Moreira Mendes (PUC-MG)
	Eliete Correia dos Santos (UEPB)
	Fabiano Santos (UERJ/IESP)
	Francinete Fernandes de Sousa (UEPB)
	Francisco Carlos Duarte (PUCPR)
	Francisco de Assis (Fiam-Faam, SP, Brasil)
	Jacques de Lima Ferreira (UP)
	Juliana Reichert Assunção Tonelli (UEL)
	Maria Aparecida Barbosa (USP)
	Maria Helena Zamora (PUC-Rio)
	Maria Margarida de Andrade (Umack)
	Marilda Aparecida Behrens (PUCPR)
	Marli Caetano
	Roque Ismael da Costa Güllich (UFFS)
	Toni Reis (UFPR)
	Valdomiro de Oliveira (UFPR)
	Valério Brusamolin (IFPR)
SUPERVISOR DA PRODUÇÃO	Renata Cristina Lopes Miccelli
PRODUÇÃO EDITORIAL	Bruna Holmen
REVISÃO	Bruna Fernanda Martins
DIAGRAMAÇÃO	Andrezza Libel
CAPA	Kananda Ferreira
REVISÃO DE PROVA	Bruna Santos

ACKNOWLEDGMENTS

The authors would like to express their gratitude to the Postgraduate Program in Chemical and Biochemical Process Engineering (EPQB) at the School of Chemistry (EQ) of the Federal University of Rio de Janeiro (UFRJ) and the Academic Excellence Program (PROEX-CAPES), linked to EPQB, for their invaluable support.

PREFACE 1

The uncertainty about the future is impacted as much by the past as it is by the present and affects industrial processes, management practices, the supply and quality of inputs and the regulatory environment that surrounds us. It is essential to have the ability to draw possible futures, so that we can be better positioned for more assertive decision making and lower uncertainty.

The theoretical and practical work developed over the past 20 years by the Center for Industrial and Technological Studies at the Federal University of Rio de Janeiro (UFRJ) under the enlightened leadership of Prof. Suzana Borschiver, is once more offered to the general public with the publication of the second edition of this book, now with an emphasis on case studies.

The case studies illustrate the practical application of the methodology described and are examples of the strength of the theory and the value of its conclusions. Technology Roadmaps are presented in the themes of straw biogas, the application of automation technology, information, management of occupational security and safety.

The use of Technology Roadmaps is certainly the smartest way to prepare us for the diverse and potential futures be it in the industrial, governmental, or academic environments. It consists of an important tool for strategic planning, that is aligned to the status of the market, product, and technology. One's goal – and that is the usefulness of this book – is to decide today the paths that increase the probability, not only of survival, but also of remaining relevant in an increasingly uncertain future. Businessman and entrepreneurs need to familiarize themselves with the existing tools, recommended for the design of the future.

This book represents a very important contribution to society. It should be on the shelf of all who seek a deeper knowledge on 'future studies' with a technological perspective. I hope it serves an inspiration for companies all over the World.

Pedro Wongtschowski
President of the Superior Council of Innovation and Competitiveness of Fiesp

PREFACE 2

The book Technology Roadmap: Case Studies and Opportunities consolidates the leadership of Prof. Suzana Borschiver in this important area of research. Today, the decision-making process for a company to invest in a specific technology or business opportunity involves several aspects. Besides the capital and operational expenditures, the life cycle analysis of a technology, together with the knowledge of competing technologies and players are of prime importance. Thus, Technology Roadmap studies can help in this step, identifying current technologies and players in a particular subject or business opportunity, also forecasting how they may evolve within a particular time frame. Therefore, it is becoming an important tool for executives and the technical staff of companies to take decisions with respect to investments and new business opportunities.

The first chapter encompasses the philosophy and methods related to the strategic planning. In any decision-making process, the first step must involve a view of the future. In other words, it is where the company wants to be in relation to a particular technology or position in the forthcoming years. Thus, mapping the potential expectations and threats is part of the strategic planning. The chapter also highlights some of the most used methods for defining the strategic planning, such as Swot and Pestel analyses, as well as interviewing approaches, like the Delphi Method.

In chapter two, the authors describe the main theory and methods used to construct a Technology Roadmap. Besides the technology itself, a Technology Roadmap may also encompass aspects of business, strategy, and innovation, being an essential tool in the decision-making process. The types of Technology Roadmaps and the taxonomy normally used are detailed, providing a strong theoretical basis for students and professionals who want to be familiarized with this tool. In addition, some particular methodologies of Technology Roadmap creation are highlighted, including the one developed by the Neitec group at UFRJ.

The next chapters describe case studies, but also serve to showing how the theory and methods explained in the first two chapters can be used. Chapter three is focused on the Technology Roadmap for biogas production from straw. It begins with a contextualization of the topic, covering the production and uses of biogas, as well as its importance in a scenario of energy transition. Then, a detailed description of the R&D strategy, based on information available in websites, press releases, patents and articles is included, together with the most important drives that characterize the subject and that may be used to construct the Technology Roadmap, such as process, product, equipment, type of treatment and feedstock. In the sequence, a deep discussion of the Technology Roadmap is presented and associated with short, medium, and Long Terms, providing a complete view of the technologies and players related to the subject, not only in current days, but also with a view to the future.

Chapter four is dedicated to Occupational Health and Safety Management (OHS). This subject may sound out of scope for a book related with technology, but it exemplifies how broad and of general scope a Technology Roadmap can be. Initially, the chapter contextualizes what OHS is in terms of prevention, protection, and management of the work force. In this sense, sociological aspects related to OHS are discussed, taking into account data of the European Union and United States, mainly. Then, the investments in OHS were considered in terms of information and automation technologies. Thus, a brief description of the concepts of industry 4.0, big data, internet of things (IOT), machine learning and robotics are included, always relating these topics with respect to OHS. Then, the same methodology of identifying the main drivers and players, together with the potential evolution within a time frame, is applied and carefully discussed throughout the text and figures.

The fifth and last chapter of the book reports the use of Technology Roadmap in the digital transformation related to occupational health. Again, this is a topic that may be regarded as social, rather than technological in its nature, but the authors were able to identify the main trends of the digital transformation related to health issues. The concept of occupation health was discussed but focusing on digital transformation. The analysis Technology Roadmap was created following the same methodology developed by the NEITEC team, connecting the players with the drivers that were previously defined within the time frame of interest.

It is worth mentioning that each chapter covering a case study ends with a conclusion remark, which highlights the main findings and conclusions of that particular study. Overall, the book will serve as a reference guide for those interested in knowing the concepts and potential applications of Technology Roadmap studies. The book is recommended for executives and professionals of companies and governmental agencies, but it will certainly be of great importance for students who want to pursue a career in this fast-growing research area.

Claudio J. A. Mota
Professor of Chemistry and Chemical Engineering at
Federal University of Rio de Janeiro (UFRJ)

PREFACE 3

The Technology Roadmap tool enables a better understanding of technological advances over time, identification of the most promising technologies, stakeholders, and opportunities for companies and public policy formulation. Professor Suzana Borschiver and researcher Aline Tavares present an important book that outlines the main stages in drawing up and interpreting a technological roadmap. In today's world of information overload, it is crucial to have tools that can help organize and systematize knowledge to aid in decision-making.

This book features the country's top experts on the Technological Roadmap, who have provided consultancy services to various companies, organizations, and high-impact journals. It is a valuable resource that fills a significant gap in knowledge.

Pietro Adamo Sampaio Mendes
Secretary of Petroleum, Natural Gas, and Biofuels
of the Ministry of Mines and Energy (MME)

SUMÁRIO

INTRODUCTION 17

1
TECHNOLOGY ROADMAP – CASE STUDIES AND
OPPORTUNITIES 19

Marcello José Pio
Suzana Borschiver

2
TECHNOLOGY ROADMAP 41

Suzana Borschiver
Andrezza Lemos

3
TECHNOLOGY ROUTES FOR THE PRODUCTION OF BIOGAS
FROM STRAW 53

Fernanda de Souza Cardoso
Suzana Borschiver
Aline Souza Tavares

4
AUTOMATION AND INFORMATION TECHNOLOGIES
APPLIED TO OCCUPATIONAL HEALTH AND SAFETY (OHS)
MANAGEMENT 79

Aline Souza Tavares
Suzana Borschiver

5
DIGITAL TRANSFORMATION IN OCCUPATIONAL HEALTH ... 109

Suzana Borschiver
Aline Souza Tavares
Andrezza Lemos Rangel da Silva

ABOUT THE AUTHORS 135

INTRODUCTION

This book is about the second edition of the first book *Technology Roadmap: Strategic Planning to Align Market-Product-Technology*, released in 2016 by Andrezza Lemos Rangel da Silva and myself.

In the first book the focus was the construction of the technological Roadmap and in this one we will apply the methodology developed by the Nucleus of Industrial and Technological Studies (NEITEC/UFRJ), to show practical case studies, developed both in the scope of scientific research and in projects with companies and research centers.

In the first chapter, the book reviews strategic planning, future studies and methodologies, such as Swot Analysis, Scenarios, Pestel, Delphi, and Bibliometrics. In the second chapter, a review of concepts, origin, formats and methodology is also carried out.

In the third chapter, the construction of the "Technology Routes for the Production of Biogas from Straw" is presented, where the anaerobic digestion process for the synthesis of biogas is discussed, and the main results, focusing on the use of straw as raw material.

In the fourth chapter, the case study refers to the work carried out in partnership with National Industry Observatory to SESI Innovation Center on OHS Management Systems with a focus on "Automation and Information Technologies Applied to Occupational Health and Safety (OHS) Management". The concepts of Industry 4.0 such as Big Data, Internet of Things, Machine Learning and Robotics are addressed, and their applications in the work environment so that it can bring healthier and safer conditions to the worker and physical, mental and social well-being.

Finally, the fifth and last chapter deals with these technologies with a specific focus on occupational health, under the theme "Digital Transformation in Occupational Health". In partnership with SESI Viva+, an arm of the Social Service for Industry (SESI), the work addressed the use of telemedicine, wearable devices and apps, for example, to improve the management of information on workers' health in Brazilian companies.

It is hoped that this book, the result of my 20 years of experience in the areas of Technological Prospecting, Strategic Planning, Knowledge Management and Business Models, will be another contribution to the understanding of this strategic planning tool that is so important for making safe decisions in relation to the future direction of technologies and markets to be followed.

Suzana Borschiver

Full professor at the School of Chemistry – Federal University of Rio de Janeiro (UFRJ)

1

TECHNOLOGY ROADMAP – CASE STUDIES AND OPPORTUNITIES

Marcello José Pio
Suzana Borschiver

1.1 Strategic planning, future studies and methodologies

Make time to think. The speed of change should not be an
excuse for a lack of strategy.
(Michael Porter)

To manage is to forecast and plan, to organize, to command,
to co-ordinate, and to control.
(Henry Fayol)

Strategic planning has been one of the most important management issues. One of the most relevant names in the sector, Henry Fayol, quotes that "managing means looking ahead". The objective of strategic planning is to look to the future and anticipate needs and demands, offering efficient answers to face problems and control risks and uncertainties, and thus generate a direction considered adequate for the organization. Strategic planning can be considered a management tool that enables the establishment of the course to be followed by a company, aiming at achieving a level of optimization in its relationship with the environment.

This look to the future has been a constant exercise by organizations to prepare to surpass their competitors and, therefore, conquer space in the competitive environment. Since it is not possible to predict the future with 100% accuracy, reflections on threats and opportunities are supported and guided by varied techniques and studied with greater consistency and application specificity.

Decisions are based on the expectation of holding an event or situation. Thus, it can be said that to decide is to take a stand in relation to the future. Depending on the time available for decision making and the volume of information that can be obtained within that period, the individual will stand between the state of certainty, when his decision is unique and of a deterministic character; or uncertainty, when it will depend on a set of hypotheses of a probabilistic character. The future, besides being inevitable, is uncertain. However, it is possible to predict some future events because of past acts and decisions or subject to a regular calendar (Santos, 2004).

The literature presents two types of future models: extrapolative (forecasting) and exploratory (foresighting). The exploratory model is based on evaluating the evolution of a given quantity over a period, considering a certain degree of confidence/probability. In this model, future hypotheses are proposed based on these data. In the extrapolative model, projections are created from the extension of a past evolution.

The literature points out those extrapolative techniques are nowadays understood as simpler in terms of conceptual understanding and in relation to their application in practical cases. In face of this, they have become widespread among professionals in different areas of knowledge. Despite their simplicity and dissemination, such models are not always effective as forecasting resources, as they sometimes need to be combined with other techniques and approaches. This is because in general, forecasting models require data that are based on the premise that the future will look like the past, which, in reality, does not always happen. In addition, it is known that, in most cases, databases, when available, are unreliable, incomplete or without periodicity of updating, with different measurement units and little data relevant to the study. However, extrapolation on past trends relies mostly on reliable historical data, which should cover a relatively long period, preferably longer than the projected period, and with uniform patterns of collection over time. Despite presenting limited applications, this approach brought historical contributions to the subject. However, in many cases, it should be replaced by alternatives that are more suitable. Reflections of this nature allowed a better adaptation of methodologies and tools to the objects of study, leading consequently, to the definition of new concepts. The exploratory alternative (forecasting) mentioned above shows greater adherence to the foresight approach, or foresight, discussed below.

According to Cuhls and Grupp (2001), foresight can be defined as a

> Process that systematically seeks to examine the long-term future of science, technology, economy, and society, aiming at identifying areas of strategic research and emerging generic technologies that tend to generate the greatest economic and social benefits.

While narrowing the focus on the Long Term, this definition is broad across its sectors of application. Subjectively, it considers the decision-making process as a central aspect of foresighting. This same factor is explicitly presented in Marcial and Grumbach´s approach (2006), where foresighting is an ongoing process of thinking about the future thus identifying elements for better decision-making and taking into consideration the economic, social, environmental, scientific, and technological aspects.

As for the characteristics, Godet's (1982) foresight studies involve understanding the phenomenon as a whole (nothing remains the same); variables (qualitative, not necessarily quantifiable, subjective, known or hidden); relationships (dynamic, with evolving structures); explanation (the future is the "raison d'être" of the present); future (multiple and uncertain); method (intentional analysis, with qualitative and stochastic models); and attitude towards the future (active and creative). As they constitute the focus of prospective exercises, definitions of technological prospecting are also presented, aiming to broaden the understanding of the subject. Technological prospecting is the term applied to studies that aim to anticipate and understand the potential, evolution, characteristics, and effects of technological changes, particularly its invention, innovation, adoption, and use.

For Kupfer and Tigre (2004), technology foresight is the systematic means of mapping future scientific and technological developments, capable of significantly influence an industry, economy, or society.

1.2 Technological Planning and Technology Foresight

Technological planning is the key to increasing competitiveness. Its objective is to guide the company in the acquisition, development, and application of technology in a strategic way to obtain a technological advantage and suited to the strategic objectives of the entire company. For a company, having an R&D department with all the necessary equipment and qualified researchers is not enough. It is necessary that strategic processes support operational excellence to allow technology foresight techniques to be the key to technological management since they can anticipate trends, contributing to decision-making, resource allocation, risk analysis and the definition of technical competencies to be developed.

According to Porter *et al.* (1991, p. 9) in affirming national competitiveness, the company is the center of the action, because in capitalist economies the company is usually the one who must deliver the technology.

The author presents a structure for technological development in a company considering external (cultural, political, and economic) and internal aspects (scientific and technological resources, R&D funds, patents, and all production factors and product development, such as capital, materials, work, equipment etc.). According to this model, technology management starts with R&D.

Product portfolio development should be done as a way to ensure that investments are properly allocated. Furthermore, to prioritize their investments, companies must understand technology and market trends through technology strategy.

Technology foresight is also of great value in guiding the development of a promising technology. Their value lies in their usefulness in making better decisions, not in becoming real. In other words, technology foresight is typically an approximation of the future and must not encompass all its real forms. It aims not only to identify gaps in knowledge and research to find ways to reach an objective but also to map the challenges that will be encountered in the future.

Studies of this nature seek to reveal a specific characteristic or attribute of technology in a given period. Joseph Martino defines technological foresight as a future prediction of the use of machines, procedures, and techniques. During the 1950s-60s, technological foresight was mainly driven by military competition between the United States and the Soviet Union (Coates *et al.*, 2001; Porter, 1999). It was initially used as a tool to aid in anticipating needs in military technology and to aid in the planning and prioritization of R&D and development systems (Porter, 1999). Hal Linstone pointed out that technology foresight reached its peak around 1970, with methodological advances from that time onwards (Coates *et al.*, 2001).

Since the 1960s, long-term planning has been widely used by companies, due to the growth of competition between them, added to the speed of technological change and the rapid advancement of information technology (Payne, 1971; Fulmer; Rue, 1974). In the second half of the 1960s, Erich Jantsch and Robert Ayres Erich described that companies began to focus on integrating technology foresight with long-term planning and its implications for organizational and operational structures. The analysis of the environment is at the junction of foresight, forecast, and strategy. The business community has focused on environmental studies such as trend analysis using bibliometrics and patents (Martino, 2003; Porter; Detampel, 1995) and market analysis to identify the growing diversification of consumer needs (Fahey *et al.*, 1981) to establish an understanding of technology initiatives as well as improve their future position. Additionally, the company must adjust its R&D strategy in alignment with its business strategies, such as manufacturing, sales, and marketing, human resources, finance, and accounting. Many companies have researched disruptive technologies, technological improvements, and technologies that define the state of the art. Today, more than ever, the identification of a technology foresight tool for decision-making is necessary to predict future trends.

Literature and management practices have identified numerous techniques for technology foresight studies and among them are Swot Analysis; scenarios; Pestle analysis; interviews; focus group and market research; Delphi technique; cross-impact technique; bibliometric analysis; theory of inventive problem solving (Triz); Technology Roadmap. In the next item, we will briefly present each of these techniques.

1.3 Technology Foresight Techniques

1.3.1 Swot Analysis

The Swot analysis (Strength, Weakness, Opportunity, Threats) aims to assess the internal and external factors that influence an organization. Internal factors are called strengths and weaknesses. Strengths are resources or capacity of the organization that can be used effectively to achieve its goals. Weaknesses are limitations, failures, or defects in the organization that make it difficult to achieve its goals. Some authors consider that the strength of an organization can turn into a weakness, as long as the context of a given external environment is changed.

External factors are defined as opportunities and threats. Opportunities are trends in situations or events external to the organization, which can help it achieve its objectives and mission. Threats are trends in situations or events that can harm the organization in pursuit of its objectives and mission. The identification of external factors must consider the effects and their consequences, the probability and estimated time for the occurrence.

Once identified the internal and external factors, will be analyzed in a matrix (Figure 1), seeking to verify the existence of a relationship between them.

Figure 1 – Matrix of Strengths, Opportunities, Weaknesses, Threats

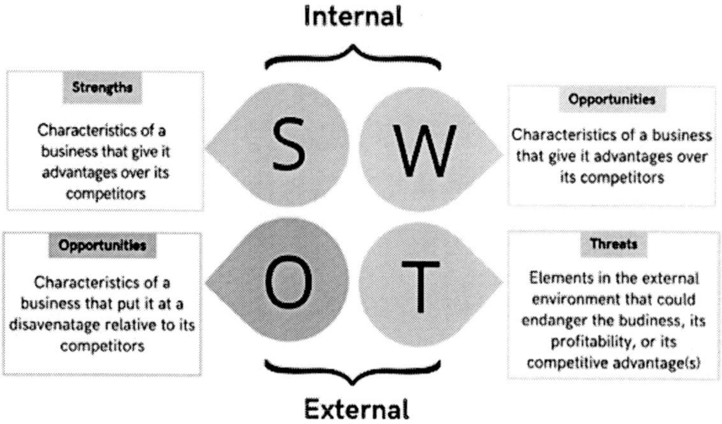

Internal

Strengths

Characteristics of a business that give it advantages over its competitors

S **W**

Opportunities

Characteristics of a business that give it advantages over its competitors

Opportunities

Characteristics of a business that put it at a disavenatage relative to its competitors

O **T**

Threats

Elements in the external environment that could endanger the budiness, its profitability, or its competitive advantage(s)

External

Source: own elaboration from Peterdy (2022)

Strengths and weaknesses are placed on the horizontal lines, respectively. Opportunities and threats are placed on vertical lines. The degree of impact intensity can be indicated either by numbering (3 – strong impact, 2 – medium impact, 1 – low impact, 0 – no impact) or by letters (A – high impact, M – medium impact, B – low impact and N – no impact). From the generated quadrants, it can be considered that quadrant I demonstrate a potential for offensive action by the organization, as it can take advantage of existing opportunities through its strengths. Quadrant II demonstrates the organization's defensive capacity, capable of neutralizing or minimizing threats through its strengths. Quadrant III indicates the organization's weak points, as its weaknesses prevent it from taking advantage of envisioned opportunities. Quadrant IV shows the organization's vulnerability points, that is, the threats that may be implemented due to identified weaknesses in the organization.

Swot analysis helps guide quickly, from focus to scenario analysis, showing which areas of the environment are most critical to the organization.

1.3.2 Scenarios

Foresight studies can be supported by a set of scenarios, which aim to cover the possibilities of certain events, players, or systems. Its use in prospective studies was initiated in the 1960s by Herman Kahn in the USA, and by the *Delegation à l'amenagement du territoire et à l'action régionale* (Datar) in France. Scenarios are sets formed by describing future situations. A scenario is a sequence of hypothetical events, built with the aim of focusing on the determining processes as well as critical issues for decision-making. Scenarios are defined as reasonable and feasible sets of possible futures properly structured. They are built through the various interpretations of the events that guide the structure of the business environment, enabling companies to "rehearse the future", thus seeking to anticipate and understand risks and identify strategic options not yet seen.

Scenarios are important as a source of learning in an organization, as they manage to unify the most diverse and different views, thus generating common strategic thinking, from the intermediate levels to decision-makers, which implies more coherent strategic planning. The scenarios can be divided into:

Exploratory: Consider past and present trends, which in turn lead to the creation of feasible futures. Emphasizing the indeterminacy of the future, exploratory scenarios work with the complexity of exogenous factors to determine possible alternatives for the future. They aim to describe, conceptually and qualitatively, the possibilities of the evolution of present events. However, there can be no assurance that some of these possibilities will occur.

Normative or Anticipation: These scenarios are built based on alternative images of the future. They can be divided into desired or feared. The basic characteristic of these scenarios is to consider that the future can be built with the application of power. They are commonly used by state planning organizations.

Trend: In this type of scenario, the future is determined through the interpretation of current trends of the variables that affect social, technological, economic, political, and cultural factors. Analogous to the trend future, these scenarios consider that such factors will not change, and the future is, consequently, similar to the past.

1.3.3 Pestel Analysis

The Pestel analysis, which has its name based on an acronym formed by the first letters of key factors when analyzing a situation. A tool based on Macro Environmental factors. Assumes that the business success of a company should not be understood or studied without first analyzing and understanding all the existing information related to a better understanding of the external organizational environment. This type of analysis is intended to help the company understand and react to changes in its external environment.

The **P** refers to Political factors, that is, aspects inherent to state interventions in economic, licensing, and government controls that may exist. **E** deals with Economic factors, macro, and micro aspects that impact the external environment, related to the type of seasonal demand, weather factors, and others. O **S** are the Social, cultural, and demographic factors of the external environment and its impacts. The **T** is the Technological factors, thus understood with the infrastructure, innovations, and their impacts related to the technology involved. The **S** refers to Social aspects, referring to work relations, the communities involved, and relevant factors in relation to the human factor and its relationships. Finally, the **L** refers to the Legislation, at the different levels, federal, state, and municipal: environmental licensing, patents, licensing, operating authorization etc.

Visual tools are interesting for applying the methodology. One example is the use of Canvas, a generic name for a group thinking technique that uses a vertical surface, such as a whiteboard and slips, to place items arranged in delimited areas of this vertical surface. Figure 2 shows an example for building a Pestel analysis using Canvas.

Figure 2 – Canvas structure for Pestel analysis

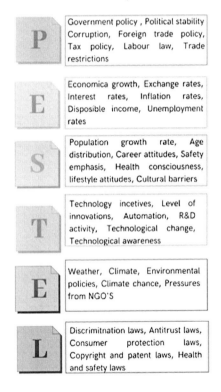

Source: own elaboration from Bruin (2016)

1.3.4 Interviews

The interview technique is relevant to access tacit knowledge. It is used when looking for more complex and precise information. Through interviews, it is possible to obtain information that is not contained in official documents, but that may be relevant to the study's conclusions. Interviews follow a standard method by which questions are pre-set. Below, some basic rules for having a good interview process are highlighted:

- Start the interview by explaining your goals.

- Explain the purpose of the information generated and ensure the anonymity of the organization and the person interviewed.

- Do not ask specific pre-elaborated questions, but generic questions that can be used as starting point for possible new questions.

- Listening effectively and interactively.

- Generate an environment of trust between interviewee and interviewer.

- Do not record the interview.

1.3.5 Focus group and market research

The focus group, although it finds its historical roots in Robert King Merton, more precisely in the year 1941, is a way of collecting data that only from the 1980s onwards developed more intensely as an important research strategy on the part of social scientists.

The Focus group, also known as a discussion group, is a technique that aims to collect data through the interaction of a group on a certain topic presented by the mediator, which can be used at different times in the research process.

When structuring the focus group, it is necessary to be concerned not only with the selection of participants but also with the way in which the collected data will be handled, that is, with the information given in confidence to the moderator/investigator.

These points are decisive for group's constitution, as they are related to the profile of the participants, the size of each group, the number of groups to be worked on, and the level of intervention of the moderator. This relationship of trust between the individuals who participate in the group and the moderator/investigator must ensure anonymity and confidentiality. In addition, before any procedure, it is essential that the issue to be addressed be well defined, even if preliminary.

The option to build the problem with the group participants is valid, although it requires other precautions that will be addressed later when the possibility of conciliation with other techniques/ methods will be discussed. Once the criteria and variables that will guide the constitution of the focus group have been defined, it is important that the segmented design of the groups strive for the balance between homogeneity and heterogeneity, as a general criterion. For example, if individuals of a group are part of an adult education program (homogeneity criterion), the constitution of the groups can consider differences in age, sex, geographic origin, among others. These variables will be defined according to the nature of the problem to be investigated. Individuals with common characteristics therefore, form focus groups. A balance between uniformity and diversity of the group must be ensured.

1.3.6 Delphi

The Delphi method was developed by Olaf Helmes, in the 1960s, and consists of asking a group of experts individually and using pre-elaborated questionnaires, about the future trend of a particularly critical factor, system, or part of a system. The Delphi technique is based on the principle that several heads are better than one when seeking subjective conjectures about the future and the participants will elaborate conjectures based on rational judgments and not simply guesswork. The Delphi technique is a process of exploring future opportunities, which aims to seek a consensus through a combination of questions from qualitative and quantitative structures.

The Delphi technique is used in judgmental and prospecting circumstances when classical statistical models are not viable due to an alleged discontinuity of historical, economic, and technical information and data. In this case, information from human judgment observations and inferences is needed. Four basic points can characterize the Delphi technique: anonymity, interaction, exchange of information, and statistical control of the answers given. Anonymity is achieved through structuring and sending questionnaires to the interviewee. This "isolation" is important to obtain the opinion of each expert individually and not through a group discussion process. In addition, this procedure allows each expert to express himself without the interference of possible "social pressures", such as, for example, the influence of the opinion of a group or of another renowned expert.

Questions are posed in several rounds. Once analyzed, and rephrased, the experts can re-evaluate their first opinion and try to reach common sense. The method seeks to converge experts' opinions and raise certain commonalities on consistent issues. The Delphi method is composed of two working groups. The group of experts is made up of people who are recognized for their intense knowledge of one part of the studied system, their superficial knowledge of other parts of the system, and their keen interest in participating in such studies. The level of knowledge of each specialist can be explained by him/her when asking a specific question about a certain part of the system under study. The control group or researcher aims to manage the judgment of values issued by experts through the opinions collected, seeking not to alter or mischaracterize them, and thus prepare the synthesis of the conclusions and the final format of the work. Due to its interactive nature, the possible dispersion that may exist regarding the experts' answers may be reduced until reaching a consensus, through the feedback of information to the experts. Therefore, each expert will have the possibility to review their starting positions at each round of questions.

The Delphi method can be divided into three phases. In the first phase, the study area is defined and the first questionnaire is prepared. It should be noted that Delphi studies are typically conducted with at least three rounds. The elaboration of the questionnaire must consider some fundamental characteristics. Questions must be accurate, quantifiable, and independent.

The second phase is the selection of experts who will participate in a prospecting study. The experts must be chosen for their ability to foresee future scenarios. Normally, most studies that use this technique work with a range of 15 to 20 experts per each study, and many of them can contribute many ideas, thus hindering the contextualization process.

Generally, a hierarchy of knowledge about the subject at hand is created, usually assuming algebraic values. The levels are divided into:

- High: At this level, all specialists who hold knowledge on the subject or topic are considered.

- Medium: At this level, all specialists who have a good knowledge of the subject are taken into account but are not experts.

- Low: This level includes all specialists who have knowledge of the subject through specialized literature.

From the open questions of the first questionnaire, the researcher(s) structure the topics. The second questionnaire is developed based on the information collected during the first round.

During the second round, experts are asked to review all items identified in the first round. Experts can use a value scale or rank items to establish a preliminary priority between them. At this stage, experts are invited to comment on the reasons for the benefits and add other topics. During the third round, and any other rounds needed, the experts re-evaluate each item.

To aid their considerations, participants can be provided with: (a) feedback with statistical information on the values assigned to each item by the evaluator himself; (b) the average assigned to each item by the group; (c) a summary of the comments made by each expert.

This feedback allows experts to know the values assigned to each opinion and the underlying reasons that led each expert to assign those values. Note that typically Delphi rounds continue until a predetermined level of consensus is reached or no new information is added; in most cases, three rounds are enough.

In the second round of questions, experts are confronted with a comparative table with values assigned by themselves and the group average. From this point on, experts are invited to reflect on the values given and, if they wish, modify the values previously assigned. If necessary, there will be other rounds of questions, when each expert will be invited to comment on the divergent arguments until a median consensus is reached.

The main advantages of the Delphi method can thus be determined:

- It brings together people from a wide geographic area, avoiding creating committees, which can be disadvantageous.

- Suppress the influence of status and personality power among guest experts.

- Final consensus due to question rounds.

- Obtaining information on the future evolution of the issue in question, through present events, trends, and determinant rupture.

- Possibility of using the methodology in various fields of knowledge (economics, politics, technology, and social sciences).

- Guarantee of confidentiality of opinion.

- However, some critical points must be observed in the Delphi method:

- Depending on the complexity of the area studied and the variety of topics proposed, the time spent preparing the questionnaire can be extensive. The criteria for identifying and selecting experts must be well established.

- "Scholars from the same area of knowledge tend to think equally, which can make them reach a consensus, without considering all the relevant factors." From the first questionnaire, the process of adapting the experts' answers for use in subsequent rounds can lead to imprecision in translating the experts' opinions. It is possible not to know enough about thought trends when considering future events.

In technology foresight studies using Delphi, the following advantages are observed: It encourages the scientific and technological community to think periodically about future technological trends and their relationship to the most intense social, political, and economic priorities and challenges. Relate trends to future demands for innovation, due to the participation of experts from the business, academic, and government fields. Consider all aspects of science and technology, contributing to the global understanding of specific topics. Promote relationships between the government, private and academic sectors, through the exchange of information and opinions on the future of science and technology in the medium and Long Term.

1.3.7 Cross-impact technique

The Cross Impact Techniques were implemented to complement the results obtained by the Delphi method. This technique consists of simulation to analyze the causal relationships between events. The Delphi method is deficient, as it does not consider the interaction between factors or events. On the other hand, the cross-impact analysis considers that the occurrence of a certain variable or event will depend, to a greater or lesser extent, on the occurrence of other variables or events. Cross-impact techniques seek to determine the most likely scenarios among the possible ones.

They can be used after the application of Delphi and aim to question specialists about the impacts of the occurrence of each event on the others. Therefore, the absolute probabilities achieved using Delphi are "transformed" into conditional probabilities.

Among the cross-impact techniques, the cross-impact matrix developed by Helmer and Dalkey is considered an efficient tool for determining and analyzing the critical factors of a system or organization, as is limited to detailing probabilities and estimating effects. This technique is a tool for organizing factors as well as internal and external variables, and their respective effect relationships, seeking to provide a basis for building scenarios. In addition to analyzing the degree of dependence between factors or variables, the cross-impact matrix can also determine the factors or variables that exert greater criticality on the system or organization (driving factors) and those of greater dependence. Driving factors are those with the ability to drive an organization or system, as they significantly affect all factors of relevance to the system or organization.

1.3.8 Bibliometric analysis

One of the means most used by the scientific community to disseminate research results is the publication of articles in scientific journals. The results of scientific research need to be formally disclosed to ensure the authorship of those who developed them. Thus, the scientific article, due to its condition as a source of original and quality information, constitutes a vehicle for transmitting the knowledge produced by researchers, serving as base literature to corroborate existing studies and inspire new research.

Bibliometrics is a quantitative analysis method for scientific research that makes it possible to observe the state of science and technology through all scientific production registered in a data repository.

It allows situating a country in relation to the world, an institution in relation to a country, and individual scientists in relation to the scientific community. It is based on counting scientific articles, patents, and citations.

Depending on the purpose of the bibliometric study, the data can be either the text that makes up the publication as well as the elements present in records extracted from bibliographic databases, such as authors' names, title, source, language, keyword, classification, and quotes.

Bibliometrics can help identify trends in knowledge in a given area of knowledge, dispersion and obsolescence of scientific fields, as well as more productive authors and institutions, and journals most used in the dissemination of research in a given area of knowledge. Production indicators are useful for the planning and execution of public policies, as well as for the scientific community's knowledge of the system in which it operates.

1.3.9 Theory of inventive problem solving (Triz)

Triz arose from the work of GS Altshuller, born in Tashkent, Russia, on October 15, 1926, and died in Baku, Azerbaijan, on September 24, 1998. It is Altshuller who owes the credit for the creation of Classical Triz. Started in the 1940s, Triz is the Russian acronym for Rechénia Izobretátelskih Zadátchi Theory and stands for Inventive Problem Solving Theory. According to Altshuller, inventive problems are a special kind of problem and one that contains contradictions. The acronym Triz emerged in the 70s, being adopted internationally. Triz is a systematic methodology, oriented to the human being. It is knowledge-based for inventive problem solving and organizational learning. Triz is dedicated to inventive problem-solving. Although today it is applied in the most diverse areas of knowledge (administration, advertising, arts), this methodology was initially developed for engineering and its initial purpose was to develop a method for inventing.

Triz is a structured methodology for innovation. With its use, the organizations will not need to hire "creative geniuses" or rely only on intuitive processes to solve their problems, like for example, brainstorming.

For Altshuller, a problem-solving theory should be:

- A systematic, step-by-step procedure;
- A guide through the totality of known solutions, to the ideal solution;
- Repeatable, reliable and independent of psychological tools;

- Allow access to the knowledge base of inventive solutions;
- Allow adding to the knowledge base of inventive solutions;
- Be familiar to inventors, thus following the regular creation process.

Triz is based on some basic principles such as technique, contradiction, evolution, resources and ideality:

- TECHNIQUE – The systematic study of techniques and their functions is the basis and foundation of Triz. The definition of technique depends on the definitions of a technical system (TS) and technological process (TP). Any artificial object, regardless of its nature or degree of complexity, can be considered a technical system. Any artificial action or consequence of procedures for carrying out an activity assisted by a technical system can be considered a technological process.

- CONTRADICTIONS – Occur when an improvement in one parameter or characteristic of a technique negatively affects other parameters or characteristics of other techniques. The correct formulation of contradictions is the basis for starting an inventive solution.

- FIELD-SUBSTANCE RESOURCES – These are part of the technique and can be used to perform their own functions. Resources can be classified as natural or environment, time, space, system, substance, field/energy, and information.

- TECHNICAL EVOLUTION – Most technical systems change over time. This change can occur through gradual development or through leaps or revolutions. Development happens when new requirements or new parameters are needed. This long-term change is called technical evolution and can follow different paths. Each of these paths can be extended to other systems, not just an engineering field. These paths are frequently repeated, which indicates the existence of system evolution rules. These rules are also called technical evolution patterns.

- IDEALITY – This principle is used to obtain a comparison parameter for the solutions found, which is the ideal solution. The ideal for Triz is to obtain an ideal machine, an ideal method, an ideal process, an ideal substance, and an ideal technique. Basically, obtaining the desired effects without mass, volume, time and space, energy, maintenance, or cost. In this sense, an ideal technique represents the maximum result, which, unfortunately, cannot be achieved, but serves as a parameter to verify how good the adopted solution is.

1.3.10 Technological mapping (Technology Roadmap)

In the view of technology foresight and its tools, it is possible to insert the Roadmap with great prominence for its performance. This tool is advantageous for its comprehensiveness and versatility, as, in addition to analyzing the environment, it also enables monitoring of competitors over time, establishes market trends, studies technological trajectories, company profiles, and identifies opportunities for new business.

Technology Roadmapping (TRM) is a corporate planning and management technique used to align organizational goals and technological resources in manufacturing and service companies. It constitutes an important method to trigger collaborative technological planning. Its application in companies worldwide is a dynamic process, which enables the experience of people to work together and trace paths to reach their goals. This will be the methodology detailed in the next chapter.

REFERENCES

ALVARES, Lillian Maria Araujo de Rezende; ITABORAHY, Anderson Luis Cambraia (org.). **Os múltiplos cenários da informação tecnológica no Brasil do século XXI**. Brasília, DF: IBICT; UNESCO, 2021.

BORN, Jeferson Carlos. **Recuperação Da Teoria Do Planejamento Estratégico, Especialização em Desenvolvimento Econômico da**

Universidade Federal do Paraná. Curitiba, 2012. Disponível em: https://acervodigital.ufpr.br/bitstream/handle/1884/50938/R%20-%20E%20-%20JEFERSON%20CARLOS%20BORN.pdf?sequence=1&isAllowed=y. Acesso em: 1 set. 2022.

BRUIN, L. De. **Scanning the Environment:** PESTEL Analysis. Disponível em: https://www.business-to-you.com/scanning-the-environment-pestel-analysis/. Acesso em: 1 set. 2022.

CHO, Yonghee; YOON, Seong-Pil; KIM, Karp-Soo. An industrial technology Roadmap for supporting public R&D planning. **Technological Forecasting & Social Change**, v. 107, 2016, p. 1-12.

GALEGO, Carla; GOMES, Alberto A. Emancipação, ruptura e inovação: o "focus group" como instrumento de investigação. **Revista Lusófona de Educação**, v. 5, 2005, p. 173-184. Disponível em:https://revistas.ulusofona.pt/index.php/rleducacao/article/view/1012. Acesso em: 1 jun. 2023.

MANNARELLI FILHO, Teucle. **Análise de Posicionamento Estratégico e Consolidação da Marca em Commodity de Silvicultura:** Um Estudo de Caso em Empresa Integrada e Verticalizada no Estado do Mato Grosso do Sul; XIV Simpósio de Excelência em Gestão e Tecnologia, 2017. Disponível em: https://www.aedb.br/seget/arquivos/artigos17/242516.pdf. Acesso em: 1 jun. 2023.

PETERDY, K. **SWOT Analysis**. Disponível em: https://corporatefinanceinstitute.com/resources/knowledge/strategy/swot-analysis/. Acesso em: set. 2022.

PIMENTEL, Andrey Ricardo P. **Considerações sobre triz e sua aplicação no desenvolvimento de software.** Centro Federal de Educação Tecnológica do Paraná. Curitiba, [S.n.]. Disponível em: https://www.inf.ufpr.br/andrey/publicacoes/trizartigo.pdf. Acesso em: 1 jun. 2023.

PIRES, Jose Geraldo Carlos. **Metodologia Triz uma Opção para Solução de Problemas Orientada Ao Ser Humano e Estruturada para Inovação.** XI Simpósio de Excelência em Gestão e Tecnologia, 2014. Disponível em: https://www.aedb.br/seget/arquivos/artigos14/2720384.pdf. Acesso em: 1 jun. 2023.

SILVA, Isabel Soares Silva; VELOSO, Ana Luísa Veloso; KEATING, José Bernardo. Focus group: Considerações teóricas e metodológicas. **Revista Lusófona de Educação**, v. 26, p. 175-190. Disponível em: https://www.redalyc.org/pdf/349/34931782012.pdf. Acesso em: 1 jun. 2023.

SILVEIRA JUNIOR, Luiz A. Bloem; VASCONCELLOS, Eduardo; GUEDES, Liliana Vasconcellos; GUEDES, Luis Fernando A.; COSTA, Renato Machado. Technology Roadmapping: A methodological proposition to refine Delphi results. **Technological Forecasting & Social Change**, v. 126, 2018, p. 194-206.

SOARES, Patrícia Bourguignon; CARNEIRO, Teresa Cristina Janes; CALMON, João Luiz; CASTRO, Luiz Otávio da Cruz de Oliveira. Análise bibliométrica da produção científica brasileira sobre Tecnologia de Construção e Edificações na base de dados Web of Science. **Ambiente Construído**, Porto Alegre, v. 16, n. 1, p. 175-185, jan./mar. 2016. Disponível em: https://www.scielo.br/j/ac/a/7CmZ3n8FT8R5g93DkW5kzMJ/abstract/?lang=pt. Acesso em: 1 jun. 2023.

2

TECHNOLOGY ROADMAP

Suzana Borschiver

Andrezza Lemos

The concept of a Technology Roadmap can encompass several meanings. Some authors refer to the technological Roadmap as a visual resource that links research and development programs, capabilities, and specific requirements. Others define it as an unfolding map of technological evolution and the products that implement them. The term "technological Roadmap", therefore, is widely used, although there is no uniqueness regarding its definition. As such, there are variations on what the technological Roadmap delivers among its users.

In fact, technology is just one aspect of the Roadmap and the most general approach to the term should be a business, strategic, or innovation Roadmap, although "technological Roadmap" is the most used term.

The generic Roadmap is a multi-layered, multi-temporal graph. Many types of Roadmaps have been used and the existing literature has tried to classify them into different categories. Sandia National Laboratories presented one of the most common categorizations. There are three types of Roadmaps comprising product Technology Roadmap, issue-specific Roadmap, and emerging technologies Roadmap. Albright and Kappel point out four sessions namely, Market, Product, Technology, and Action Plan considered when constructing the Roadmap. Several Roadmap templates are introduced to build a product evolution map, product, technological, risk, and strategic action map. Phaal *et al.* examined a group of approximately 40 Technology Roadmaps and grouped them into clusters in 16 areas. In addition, at least a dozen different Roadmap applications were presented at a workshop held in 1998, which can be broadly classified into four groups, including science and technology map, industrial technology map, corporate or product technology map and product and portfolio management map, according to their applications and objectives. Finally, Kappel suggested a Roadmapping taxonomy based on the purpose and emphasis of the map. As a result, a large number of Roadmaps have been divided into four groups, which are science and Technology Roadmaps, product Technology Roadmaps, industrial Roadmaps, and product Roadmaps (Lee; Park, 2005).

The most widely used framework for science and technology (S&T) Roadmap links market, product, and technology. There are other examples such as Market-Product-Technology-Project R&D and Market-Product-Technology-Science. The aim of building a S&T Roadmap is to think of products at the right time, driven by the external environment, such as market trends, the conduct of suppliers and competitors, and social changes.

It is necessary to adapt internal resources and the R&D project to the accomplishment of the final product. Roadmapping becomes an emerging field of research. The Roadmapping process involves a range of agents, from companies, industries to the global level.

2.1 Taxonomies of Roadmaps

A valuable feature of Roadmaps is their conciseness. Its visual nature has helped especially in the structured and constructive discussion of technological prospecting processes. To a better understanding of the varieties of Roadmaps found in the literature, some authors have adopted classification criteria regarding their types and formats.

Roadmaps can be presented in a variety of ways, but the most common approach is the generic Roadmap (Figure 3), which consists of a time-based graphical representation comprising a number of layers that typically include business and technology perspectives

(Phaal *et al.*, 2001). For Kappel (2001), Roadmaps should contain the key market, product, and technology parameters overtime for a part of the business.

Studies (Kappel, 2001; Garcia; Bray, 2007) suggest that the Roadmap can be represented at two levels: industrial or corporate. Some organizations apply Technology Roadmapping internally as an aspect of their technology planning (enterprise Technology Roadmapping). However, at the industrial level, Technology Roadmapping involves multiple organizations, either individually or in a consortium (industrial Technology Roadmapping).

Figure 3 – Schematic Technology Roadmap showing how technology can be aligned with product and service development, business strategy, and market opportunities

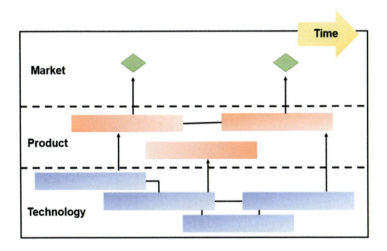

Source: own elaboration based on Phaal *et al.* (2004)

Garcia and Bray (2007) classify Roadmaps into three types as to know (i) product Roadmap, which is driven by product and/or process needs; (ii) technology-oriented Roadmap, which focuses on forecasting the development and commercialization of a new or emerging technology as well as the company's competitive position with respect to the technology and how this emerging technology and the company's competitive position will develop; and (iii) subject-oriented Roadmap, which aims to identify problems and their consequences for strategic planning and budgeting.

As for the format of Roadmaps, Albright and Kappel (2003) consider that they should have four areas, namely, market, product, technology, and action plan. Phaal *et al.* (2004) examined a set of approximately forty Technology Roadmaps and grouped them into sixteen major areas (Figure 4).

Of these sixteen major areas, eight are related to purposes of the Roadmaps (product planning, service/capacity, strategy, long term, knowledge, program, process, and integration) and eight are related to formats (multiple layers, bars, tables, graphs, figures, flowcharts, single layer, and text) of the Roadmaps.

Figure 4 – Types of Technology Roadmap classified according to purpose and format

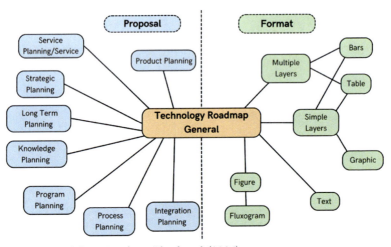

Source: own elaboration from Phaal *et al.* (2004)

The main variations of existing Technology Roadmaps in terms of purpose are described below (Phaal *et al.*, 2001, 2004).

a. Product Planning: the most common type of Technology Roadmap. It is related to the insertion of technology in manufactured products, often encompassing more than one product generation and/or product family.

b. Service/Capacity Planning: Like the first type, but more appropriate for companies offering services. It is related to the insertion of technology in the organization's capabilities.

c. Strategic Planning: typically used at the corporate level to support the assessment of changes in business drivers that result in different opportunities and threats at a strategic level.

d. Long Term Planning: usually used for sectors and/or for a nation. Widely employed by the American, Canadian, Japanese, and German governments.

e. Knowledge Planning: aimed at aligning knowledge assets and integrating knowledge management with business objectives.

f. Program Planning: aims to support the implementation and management of the strategic R&D program. This type is more related to project planning.

g. Process Planning: This recent Roadmap variation supports knowledge management focused on a specific process such as new product development management.

h. Integration Planning: directed towards the integration and/or evolution of technologies and how different technologies can be combined thus creating a new one.

Another factor that has been noted to contribute to the variety of existing Roadmaps is their graphical formats. The types of Roadmap formats are described below (Phaal *et al.*, 2001, 2004).

a. Multiple layers: is the most common format that comprises multiple layers such as technology, product, and market. The evolution of each layer can be explored, along with the connection between sub-layers, thus facilitating integration.

b. Bars: various Roadmaps are expressed in the form of bars, both for the layer and for the sub-layer. This format has the advantage of being simple and of condensing the map outputs in order to facilitate communication, integration, and the development of software to support the Roadmap generation.

c. Tables: in some cases, tables, generally expressing the quantitative performance of the product or technology as a function of time are used throughout the entire Roadmap or in its layers.

d. Graphs: used when the performance of the product or technology can be quantified and expressed (experience curve) for each sub-layer.

e. Pictures: some Roadmaps use creative ways to represent and communicate the integration by using pictures such as trees to represent the evolution of products and technologies.

f. Flowcharts: it is a specific type of figure in the form of a flow, representing objectives, actions, and outputs.

g. Single layer: this format is a variation of the multiple layers type, where a single layer is used. The disadvantage of this format is that the connection between the layers is not shown.

h. Text: Some Roadmaps are entirely, or largely, text-based and support reports, thus describing the same issue addressed in graphical formats.

Kappel (2001) suggests that the taxonomy of the document generated by the method is based on its proposal and emphasis (Figure 5), resulting in four groups of Roadmaps: (i) science/technology: aim to better understand the future, identifying trends, generating forecasting and setting development goals for the sector; (ii) industry: aim to establish technology development expectations in terms of cost and performance for the competitiveness of a sector; (iii) product-technology: seek to align product development decisions with a company's market and technology trends, and (iv) product: aim to articulate the direction and evolution schedule of a company's product and/or product families.

FIGURE 5 – TAXONOMY OF THE ROADMAP BASED ON ITS PROPOSAL AND EMPHASIS

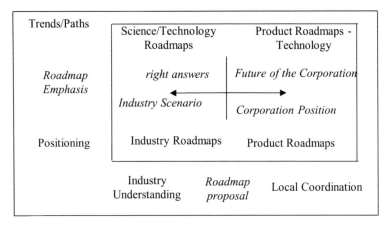

Source: own elaboration from Kappel (2001)

Figure 9 shows the horizontal axis that outlines the Roadmap proposal for the industrial or corporate levels, and the vertical axis differentiates the Roadmaps in terms of application emphasis.

2.2 T-Plan (University of Cambridge)

The objective of this approach is to establish key links between resources (technology resources) and the market (business drivers) and thus identify important gaps in market, product, and technology intelligence.

The T-Plan macrostructure consists of "planning", "Roadmapping workshops" and "roll-out" phases. These phases constitute the implementation phases of the TRM process, which in itself is incorporated in the second phase, the Roadmapping workshops (see Figure 6).

Figure 6 – TRM process, extracted and adapted from t-plan

Source: own elaboration from Phaal *et al.* (2004)

For phase II of the TRM process, Phaal *et al.* (2001, 2004) suggest a workshop-based approach, where each layer of the Roadmap is dealt with in single workshops and analysis grids are used to identify and assess the relationships between the layers and script sublayers.

The main objective of the first workshop is to identify and prioritize market and business drivers, which can be derived from the most important performance dimension, thus increasing product development. In the second workshop, the resource concepts for the product must be identified in order to satisfy the business and market drivers. After grouping these features, you determine the relationships and effects between drivers and those features using a grid. In the third workshop, technological solutions to materialize the product's characteristics are sought. After grouping resources into technical areas, their effects are discussed. The results of the three workshops point to three business areas interconnected through their respective networks. In the fourth workshop, the most suitable Roadmap is identified using the results of the previous workshops. Major milestones are determined for each sublayer (y-axis) along the time axis (x-axis). Resources such as technology programs; providers; skills, etc., are identified and paths are plotted using the results of the effect rating (ie grids) as well as by negotiation of the experts present. The main benefit of the workshop form is that it brings together key stakeholders and experts. They capture, share, and structure knowledge about the issue addressed, thus identifying strategic issues and planning the way forward.

Alongside the workshop, certain management activities are equally important and this includes facilitating other workshops, coordinating processes, and follow-up actions. Phaal *et al.* (2004) claim that many benefits are derived from the Roadmapping rather than the Roadmap itself. People from different parts of the company are brought together, thus offering an opportunity for them to share information and perspectives. Also highlighted is the TRM process as a means to support communication across the functional boundaries of the organization.

2.3 Neitec Methodology – Construction of Technological Roadmaps

In general, the Roadmap can be understood as a representation made in an organized manner, which establishes interrelationships of information arising from the study of a specific theme. Thus, as in any scientific activity, it is necessary to establish a methodology in order to systematize the procedures and guarantee the achievement of the final objective.

In this book, the methodology developed divides the construction of the Roadmap into 3 main steps, as shown in Figure 7.

Figure 7 – Methodology for the development of Technology Roadmap

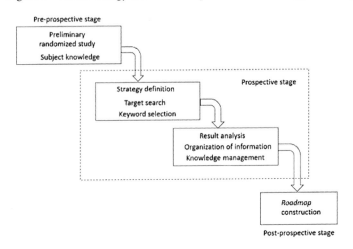

Source: own elaboration based on Borschiver and Silva (2016)

The study of any topic requires some prior knowledge from the analyst so that the selection of documents that will be studied in depth can be made with critical sense and consistency. Thus, the first stage of preparing the Roadmap is the so-called Pre-Prospective Stage, when a random search regarding the studied subject is carried out. Thus, there is an overview of the state of the art in order to define the approach used in the study and the document search strategy (keyword definition). Following this, the Prospective Stage begins with an oriented search of documents, according to the strategy defined in the previous stage. Beyond this research, the results are analyzed and the information is schematized on a database to facilitate the subsequent structuring of the Roadmap. For this, the Microsoft Excel computational framework, part of Microsoft® Office Package is commonly used. Finally, in the Post-Prospective Stage, the information previously analyzed is organized on a map, visually highlighting the most relevant aspects of the study in question, as well as the inter-relationship between the information.

REFERENCES

ALBRIGHT, R. E.; KAPPEL, T. A. Roadmapping in the corporation. **Research Technology Management**, v. 46, n. 2, p. 31-40, 2003.

BORSCHIVER, S.; SILVA, A. L. R. **Technology Roadmap** – Planejamento Estratégico para alinhar Mercado-Produto-Tecnologia, 2016.

GARCIA, M. L.; BRAY, O. H. **Fundamentals of technology Roadmapping**. Sandia National Laboratories. Disponível em: https://www.osti.gov/biblio/471364. Acesso em: jan. 2024.

KAJIKAWA, Y. *et al.* Structure of knowledge in the science and technology roadmaps. **Technological Forecasting & Social Change**, v. 75, p. 1-11, 2008.

KAPPEL, T. A. Perspectives on roadmaps: how organizations talk about the future. **The Journal of Product Innovation Management**, v. 18, p. 39-50, 2001.

LEE, S.; PARK, Y. Customization of technology roadmaps according to roadmapping purposes: Overall process and detailed modules. **Technological Forecasting & Social Change**, v. 72, p. 567-583, 2005.

PHAAL, R.; FARRUKH, C.; PROBERT, D. **T-Plan:** fast start to technology roadmapping-planning your route to success. UK: Cambridge University – Institute of Manufacturing, 2001.

PHAAL, R.; FARRUKH, C. J. P.; PROBERT, D. R. Technology roadmapping: a planning framework for evolution and revolution. **Technological Forecasting and Social Change**, v. 71, n. 1-2, p. 5-26, 2004.

3

TECHNOLOGY ROUTES FOR THE PRODUCTION OF BIOGAS FROM STRAW

Fernanda de Souza Cardoso
Suzana Borschiver
Aline Souza Tavares

3.1 Contextualization

3.1.1 Anaerobic Digestion and Biogas

In recent decades, the search for alternative energy sources has intensified due to variations in oil prices and the growing global energy demand (Fuess; Garcia, 2015). Climate changes caused mainly by the increase of gas emissions responsible for the Greenhouse Effect (GHG), along with the use of fossil fuels, have raised significant interest in fuels and chemical products generated from renewable raw materials. Biofuels derived from biomass are being promoted as low-carbon energy sources with the potential to reduce dependence on fossil fuels (Sharma, 2015).

Biogas stands out among other biofuels for its high calorific value and for being derived from a biotechnology route with high potential for technical-economic feasibility (Melendez *et al.*, 2013; Smith, 2015). This route is called anaerobic digestion and is regularly applied to the proper disposal of waste. It is a decomposition process of biodegradable organic matter in the absence of oxygen through a variety of microbial populations (Lastella, 2002). This process is popularly known as anaerobic fermentation, biomethanation, biomethanization, methanation, and methanization. Its main products are biogas, a biofuel with high calorific value and composed of approximately 60% methane and 40% carbon dioxide, and digestate, a solid residue rich in nitrogen that can be applied as a fertilizer, depending on its characteristics (Lansing, 2008).

In addition to digesters, which are reactors where the anaerobic digestion process takes place, other accessory equipment might be applied. They are temperature and pH controllers (Wang; Zou, 2012), stirrers to assist in the homogenization of solid waste (Luo *et al.*, 2016, Guo *et al.*, 2014), efficient equipment for feeding the reactor that inhibits oxygen input (Perske, G., 2012; Yue *et al.*, 2012), raw material pre-treatment equipment (Xiong *et al.*, 2015; Foody; Tolan, 2016; Jiao *et al.*, 2014a; Jiao *et al.*, 2014b), and post-treatment equipment for both the biogas and the digestate generated (Zeng; Zeng, 2016; Xu *et al.*, 2014).

Among its advantages, the low energy requirement for the operation stands out, along with no need for aeration, and less biomass production, which reduces the volume of waste generated by the treatment (Angenent *et al.*, 2004). Anaerobic processes have a high tolerance to high organic loads and the biomass can be preserved inside the digester without feeding for several months. In addition, the methane generated is collected as fuel gas rather than being released into the atmosphere. Later, it can be burned thus generating energy and converting it into carbon dioxide (Augenbraun *et al.*, 1997).

One of the requirements of anaerobic digestion is that the raw materials are bioavailable for microorganisms in anaerobic digestion. When complex raw materials are used, such as lignocellulosic waste, the application of physical, chemical, or biological pre-treatments might be necessary, thus intensifying the potential and the rate of production of methane from the biogas, improving the performance of the digester. These pretreatments aim at the delignification of biomass, reduction of cellulose crystallinity and hydrolysis of cellulose and hemicellulose into sugars, which are more bioavailable to the microbial consortium (Lalak, 2016).

The selection of a proper pretreatment is crucial for these sugars to turn into a more bioavailable form and thus increase the viability of anaerobic digestion. However, very rigorous pretreatments might lead to the formation of recalcitrant and/or toxic components, reducing the potential for methane production, and potentially making the process unfeasible (Kim, 2013; Li; Jin, 2015).

The use of lignocellulosic biomass is also a challenge due to the low concentration of available nitrogen, an important macronutrient for the functioning of the microbial organism present in the biodigester. A potential solution to balance the macronutrients, as well as moisture correction and/or dilution of inhibitory or toxic compounds, is the insertion of two or more different raw materials into the biodigester in a process called co-digestion (Mata-Alvarez *et al.*, 2011). The co-digestion of two mixed wastes offers the potential to surpass the sum of the mono-digestion of two separate wastes when it comes to the generation of methane without affecting the digestate quality, thus increasing the economic feasibility of the process (Mata-Alvarez *et al.*, 2014).

The anaerobic digestion generates two products: digestate and biogas. The generation of fertilizer or animal feed destined for the agro-industrial sector is the potential offered by the digestate. The digestate itself or its liquid fraction can also be recycled to the anaerobic digestion process, reducing the unit's water consumption (Lyu *et al.*, 2015).

Depending on the intended purpose of the biogas, there will be greater demands regarding its purity as well as its methane concentration. In order to meet the established standards, it is necessary to upgrade or post-treat the biogas. The nobler its purpose, such as the generation of bio-CNG or insertion into the gas network, the more complex and costly the upgrade will be, requiring an assessment of technical and economic feasibility for each case.

Thus, if used to produce bioenergy or biofuel, the biogas may then return to the anaerobic digestion plant in order to save on the cost of thermal and electrical energy inputs. It might also be destined for the agro-industrial sector, helping to dry grains or replacing the fuel used in harvesting machinery, or destined directly to other industries and the final consumer in the form of biomethane.

A wide range of raw materials can be used to produce biogas, such as lignocellulosic waste. Among these residues, straw stands out for its large production volume and lack of proper disposal. The large volume of patent documents on key technologies for enabling the anaerobic digestion of straw was an important driver for this work.

3.1.2 Straw

Lignocellulosic biomass is considered the most abundant organic compound in the biosphere, totaling approximately 50% of the terrestrial biomass (Pereira Jr. *et al.*, 2008) and it is present in a wide variety, from sugarcane bagasse to urban waste.

Approximately 700 million tons of agricultural waste are generated throughout China's territory annually, corresponding to more than 50% of the amount of biomass generated. Rice straw is one of the main agricultural Chinese residues, reaching up to 203 million tons per year (Luo *et al.*, 2015), followed by corn straw (Yang *et al.*, 2013).

The main residue generated from the wheat crop is straw, corresponding to 50% of the plant's weight. It is commonly used as soil cover or bedding for animals. An estimate of up to six million tons is generated from Brazilian production (Ferreira-Leitão *et al.*, 2010)

According to Santos *et al.* (2012), for each ton of sugarcane, about 140 kg of straw and 140 kg of bagasse are generated on a dry basis. In energy terms, straw represents 1/3 of the energy potential of sugarcane, which is currently underutilized. During the 2010/2011 harvest, approximately 208 million tons of sugarcane bagasse and the same amount of sugarcane straw were generated (Rocha *et al.*, 2011).

China and India are the largest rice producers, having produced 209.6 and 177.6 million tons of paddy rice in 2019, respectively (Faostat, 2021). Rice straw is a by-product of rice processing and represents about 23% of the weight of this agricultural product (Pinheiro; Gaidzinski; Souza, 2007). It is usually used for less noble purposes, such as an adsorbent in the removal of heavy metals from wastewater and/or free fatty acids from soybean oil (Nunes *et al.*, 2013).

One of the most common practices in Brazil as well as worldwide is the burning of straw in order to facilitate harvesting procedures. However, this practice releases greenhouse gas emissions into the atmosphere, such as carbon dioxide (CO_2), nitrous oxide (N_2O), methane (CH_4), and the formation of ozone (O_3), in addition to air pollution by smoke and soot (Antunes; Azania; Azania, 2013). In addition, the burning of straw in the fields can be harmful to the soil structure and the quality of new crop (Wu *et al.*, 2015).

Another practice on the rise is to throw dry leaves and pointers over the surface, forming a mulch called soil cover. This coverage undergoes physical, chemical, and biological action, benefiting the soil with nutrients and organic matter and helping to reduce the use of fertilizers. However, this practice might be just as harmful, as it emits almost twice as much nitrous oxide into the atmosphere as compared to its burning, a potent greenhouse gas 296 times greater than carbon dioxide (Juttel, 2011).

Therefore, the anaerobic digestion of straw offers the potential to simultaneously reduce environmental pollution and avoid waste of energy resources. There is a preferential generation of methane and carbon dioxide in the reactor, which will be used for energy generation or other nobler purposes. The nitrogen formed will be purified from the biogas in the form of ammonia or fixed in the digestate, which can be used as a fertilizer and return to the agricultural sector (Wu *et al.*, 2015).

The main characteristic of this type of waste is the presence of cellulose, hemicellulose, and lignin. One of the technological trends observed in recent years is the use of anaerobic digestion to provide a destination for lignocellulosic waste, which can be of agro-industrial, forestry, non-native plant species, urban waste as well as inedible plant species (Gonçalves, 2015).

Despite being a raw material with the potential for biogas generation, lignocellulose is an organic molecule with a very complex, compact, and crystalline structure for the microbial consortium to assimilate easily, as reported in anaerobic digestion (Avfall Sverige, 2012). As discussed in the previous chapter, the pretreatment of straw is crucial.

3.2 Technology Prospecting Methodology

According to the methodology for preparing Technology Roadmaps proposed under the coordination of Professor Suzana Borschiver, together with the Neitec team, the technological prospection stage began with the selection of search keywords in the databases of patents, articles, theses, technical reports, and company websites. This stage of the work was supported by two experts in the production of biogas, who reviewed the selected keywords and contributed with important insights into the biogas sector and the technologies commonly used.

Searches for documents that fulfilled the different temporal stages of the Roadmap, carried out in 2017 and 2020, according to the information detailed in Table 1.

Table 1 – R&D information search strategy

Stage	Database	Document type	Keywords
Current Stage	Biofuels Digest	Reports, websites, press releases and case study research papers	(straw or bagasse or lignocellulose or cellulose) and (biogas or anaerobic or methane)
Short Term	USPTO and Espacenet	Granted	(straw or bagasse or lign* or cellulos*) and (biogas or methane or (anaerobic and (ferment* or digest* or react*)))
Medium Term		Applications	
Long Term	Scopus	Articles, Articles in press and reviews	(straw or lign* or cellulos* or bagasse) and (biogas or "bio gas" or "marsh gas" or biomethan* or methane or methanation or methani* or "anaerobic ferment*" or "anaerobic digest*" or "anaerobic react*")

Source: own elaboration

One hundred and seven articles were found, 152 patent documents were filed, 68 granted patent documents, and 19 documents derived from specialized media. The analysis of these documents enabled the identification of similarities among them, such as the type of pretreatment applied in the straw, more common raw material, and the final product of interest. These similarities show trends in the topic under study, commonly referred to as drivers or taxonomies. The next chapter presents the main drivers identified.

3.3 Understanding the technological trends based on the elaboration and analysis of Roadmaps

The drivers selected for this study were grouped into 6 blocks, illustrated inFigure 8. The drivers can be divided into Meso and Micro. Meso drivers define the subject of the document and group them, whilst Micro drivers detail the Meso drivers, enabling their in-depth understanding and characterization.

Figure 8 – Meso and Micro drivers

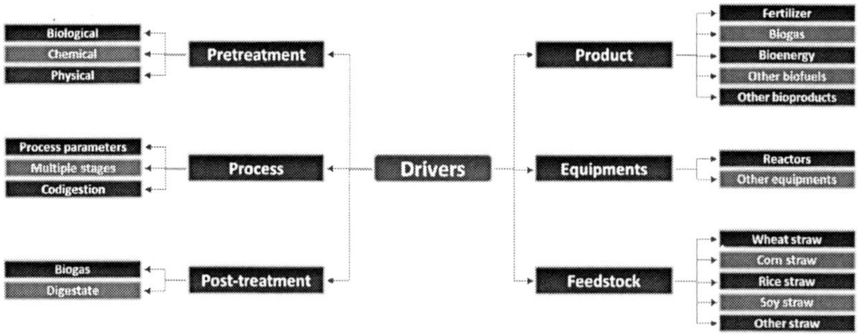

Source: own elaboration

The next items aim to analyze the relevant data that integrate the dynamics between Market, Product, and Technology involved in the production of biogas from straw, thus seeking significant relationships between companies and their markets through the results obtained in the Technology Roadmap.

In order to identify the similarities between the activities of players and their competitors in terms of R&D, as well as their markets, and the drivers involved, a vertical analysis was carried out, consisting of evaluating how players behave in a specific range, and horizontal and strategic analysis, consisting of the analysis according to their respective technological paths.

3.3.1 Vertical Analysis: Current Stage

Figure 9illustrates the cutout of the map for players acting in the "Current stage". Cluster 1, with players in the same focus of activity, is formed by Texaco Development Corporation, General Electric, and Shengli Oilfield Shengli Power Machinery. These players sell engines or products connected to these engines, such as lubricants, which run on biogas.

Shell appears on the production of lubricants for biogas engines and in the post treatment stages, with emphasis on its biogas desulphurization plant. In this regard, it resembles Xebec Adsorption Inc., which specializes in solutions for upgrading biogas, natural gas, and hydrogen. In cluster 2, the companies Du Pont and Novozymes operate in the commercialization of enzymes.

Among the players, the German company Verbio AG stands out for using straw as a raw material from local supply chains around the plant and, in exchange, supplies the owners of the surrounding lands with digestate generated as a fertilizer.

In India, Praj Industries relies on its state-of-the-art RenGasTM technology, developed with a proprietary microorganism to produce compressed biogas from rice straw. The project has annual capacity to process 35,000 metric tons of rice straw as feedstock to generate 5,250 metric tons of biogas. In addition, the project will also generate 23,000 metric tons of high quality solid digestate and 350,000 metric tons of liquid digestate for fertigation. This project has the potential to save up to 15,000 metric tons of CO_2 emissions per year (Biofuels Digest, 2021).

Meanwhile in Brazil, BNDES approved a loan of 23 million dollars for a biogas project installed in a Cocal Energia sugar plant in 2020. The project will use sugarcane straw, filter cake and vinasse to produce 33 million cubic meters per year of biogas, half of which will be used for 40,000 MWh annually of electricity production, while the rest will be upgraded to biomethane, for use in the company's own vehicles and sold to Petrobras' natural gas distributor (Biofuels Digest, 2020).

Among the Brazilian initiatives aimed at stimulating the integration of biogas in the Brazilian production chain is the Global Environment Facility (GEF) Biogás Brasil Project (GEF Biogas, 2021). Led by the Ministry of Science, Technology and Innovation (MCTI) and implemented by the United Nations Industrial Development Organization (Unido), this project has CIBiogás as its main executing agency, an institute of science and technology as an association dedicated to the development of biogas as a clean and competitive energy resource. This initiative aims to promote the renewable energy market (CIBiogas, 2021; GEF Biogas, 2021).

In a webinar held in April 2021, experts from this project presented several business opportunities focused on the use of biogas for electricity generation. According to a recent survey by CIBiogás, there was a 22% growth in the number of biogas plants in Brazil during 2020 compared to 2019, showing the national interest in this technology. In addition to the opportunities involving the electricity market, public calls involving biogas plants and the tropicalization of biogas technologies and business models between Brazilian and foreign companies stand out among potential solutions for the national sector (Brasil UN, 2021).

Figure 9 – Technology Roadmap – Current Stage

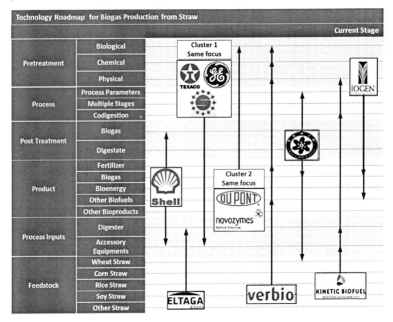

Source: own elaboration

3.3.2 Vertical Analysis: Short Term

In Figure 10, it is possible to see a cutout of the map for players operating in the "Short Term", consisting of granted patents. The Chinese Academy of Sciences research center was the major contributor to this time-lapse, with four plant-related patents in biogas production.

It can be highlighted that most documents address pretreatment technologies to increase straw bioavailability, especially physical and biological ones. Cluster 3 with the same focus, formed by Jiaxing University and the University of Warsaw, addresses biological pretreatment technologies. While the Jiaxing University patent claimed a pretreatment under aerobic conditions of straw using a microbiological preparation (CN102453676B), the University of Warsaw patent claimed a specialized microbial consortium for the pretreatment of cellulose (US9371545B2).

TECHNOLOGY ROADMAP: CASES AND OPPORTUNITIES

Figure 10 – Technology Roadmap – Short Term

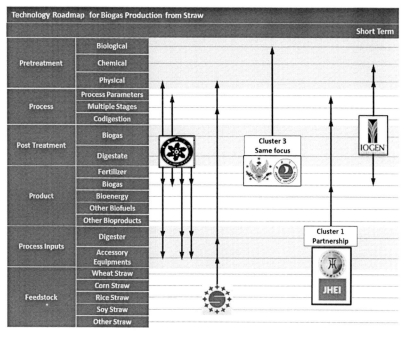

Source: own elaboration

Shengli Oilfield Shengli Power Machinery is also present in the Current Stage as a manufacturer of biogas engines, and in the Short Term is present in the claim of a process that includes a plant with a physical straw pre-treatment system, and considered a piece of accessory equipment to make it more bioavailable, followed by a multistage reaction system. The first reactor handles a high solids process and feeds the second reactor, which works with hydrocirculation to optimize methane production and generate higher quality biogas.

Cluster 1 addresses the collaboration between Jiangxi Huayifeng Ecology Industrial and Jiangxi University of Science and Technology, which aimed at co-digesting cattle waste, straw, and processed tourmaline ore. Such addition increases biogas production and the removal of the chemical demand for oxygen (CN103911397B).

Another relevant player is the Iogen Corporation, which sought the combination of unspecified physicochemical pre-treatments to extract sugary substances from cellulose-rich waste followed by a solid-liquid separation step. The liquid fraction undergoes anaerobic digestion and the solid, thermal process, for biogas production (US9476066B).

3.3.3 Vertical Analysis: Medium Term

Figure 11shows the cutout of the map for players operating in the "Medium-term", presenting information on filed patent. Novozymes has four deposited patents (IN599CHN2014A, US20140106427A1, US20130330797A1, US20130040354A1), three of them focusing only on biological pretreatment and the fourth on the three types: biological, chemical, and physical.

General Electric Corporation, which is also present in the Current Stage, claims a treatment technology that combines anaerobic digestion for the formation of biogas in the Medium Term, with post-treatment of digestate in a membrane bioreactor (MBR) to increase its stability and a 'salt concentrator' such as reverse osmosis or electrodialysis. In this way, the liquid waste generated becomes stabilized and rich in nutrients and can be used as fertilizer (WO2014098874A1).

Cluster 2, a partnership between Georgia Tech Research Corporation and Texaco claims a methodology that analyzes the crystallization index of lignocellulosic residue to predict its susceptibility to enzymatic hydrolysis ("Biological Pre-Treatment"). Through this methodology, it is possible to assess the amount of acid and heat ("Pre-Treatment – Chemical" and/or "Pre-Treatment – Physical") needed to carry out enzymatic hydrolysis, subsequently using the glucose generated for biogas production (NZ600127A).

At this stage, Shell Oil Company focuses on the pre-treatment of lignocellulosic biomass using sulfuric acid for the subsequent production of bioethanol. The liquid waste, which is rich in sulfur, is submitted to anaerobic digestion for the generation of biogas, subsequently undergoing desulfurization (US20130157334A0).

Meanwhile, the Iogen Corporation focused on chemically pretreating lignocellulosic waste with sulfuric and/or hydrogen sulfide and wet oxidation to generate waste rich in phenolic compounds, which are anaerobically digested to generate biogas and hydrogen sulfide ("Other Bioproducts"). Hydrogen sulfide can be recycled into the process (WO2016145528A1).

Figure 11 – Technology Roadmap – Medium Term

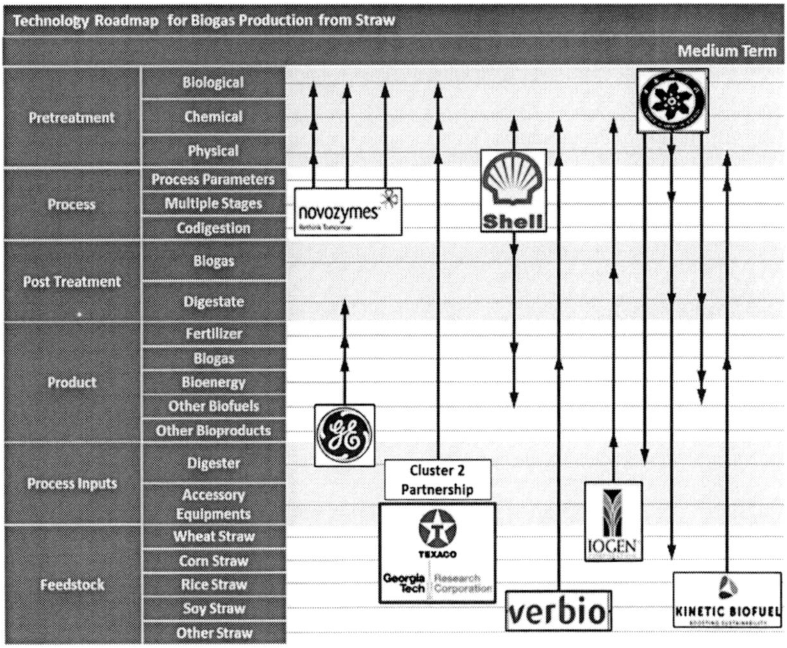

Source: own elaboration

3.3.4 Vertical Analysis: Long Term

For the Long Term, which is presented in Figure 12, information gathered from scientific articles was applied. This cutout presented the greatest expression of partnership clusters and a focus on better understanding the parameters of the process, the microbiota present in the reactor, and the co-digestion of straw with other raw materials.

The partnership Cluster 3 presents the collaboration between the Bavarian State Research Center for Agriculture and the Leibniz-Institut für Agrartechnik Potsdam-Bornim at the University Bielefeld University. This partnership provided research on a multi-stage co-digestion of straw and hay, varying process parameters, such as temperature (mesophilic and thermophilic) and pH. The evaluation was carried out through characterization and bio-marking of the medium biota.

Figure 12 – Technology Roadmap – Long Term

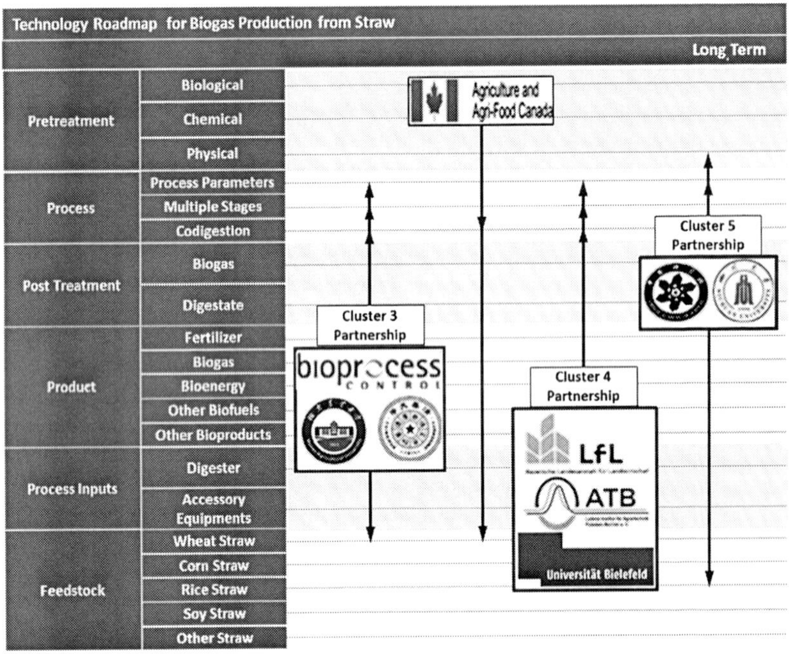

Source: own elaboration

Meanwhile, the partnership cluster 4 is formed by Xi'an Polytechnic University and the Chinese Academy of Sciences. Together, they carried out a study of the microbial community of the anaerobic digestion of different materials such as chicken litter, pig manure, cow manure, and straw. Straw alone did not present great biogas production, being superior only when compared to cow manure. It is noteworthy that the inoculum used was not stabilized and there is no evidence in the article of straw pretreatment.

The partnership cluster 5 is formed by Hunan Agricultural University and Tsinghua University together with Bioprocess control (Sweden) Co. Ltd., a leader in advanced instrumentation and control technologies. The group focused on the study of the microbial population in a multistage reactor that performs anaerobic co-digestion of wheat straw and produces waste. With microbial characterization, process parameters can be manipulated in order to optimize biogas generation.

3.3.5 Horizontal and Strategic Analysis

To complement the Roadmap's strategic analysis, horizontal analysis is necessary for a better understanding of the technological path and positioning of players over time. An example of a player is the Iogen Corporation, which develops technologies for the clean burning of second-generation biofuels, producing biogas from straw vinasse from second-generation alcoholic fermentation.

In the Short Term, the company focused on the use of physical-chemical pretreatment of straw to extract sugary substances. After solid-liquid separation, the liquid fraction is used to produce biogas and the solid fraction is used in the production of thermal energy. In the Medium Term, the same player aimed at pretreating the straw using sulfuric or hydrogen sulfide. During the anaerobic digestion process, hydrogen sulfide is generated and extracted from the biogas through a post-treatment, which is recycled to the pretreatment process. Thus, in the future, the company may seek the generation of biogas as the main straw product, and not as a co-product of 2G bioethanol.

Regarding drivers, it is possible to observe different trends over time. The "Pretreatment" driver was increasingly addressed from the Current Stage to the Medium Term in this Roadmap. This was the most prominent driver, which at the current and Short Term stage focuses on "Physical" and "Biological" processes, on chemical processes in the Medium Term, and on biological processes in the Long Term.

At the first stages cutouts, the biological process is primarily enzymatic. Players such as Novozymes and DuPont being the main highlights. However, along with other less specific pre-treatments cutouts, composting and the fungi bioaugmentation process is observed, which would tend to make the process cheaper and more accessible by reducing steps.

Maceration, crushing, and the steam explosion were the most mentioned physical pretreatments. The use of pyrolysis (by Anaergia company) was also found in some documents. As for the chemical process, there is no relevant variation over time between acidic and alkaline processes.

The main trend observed over time in the Meso driver "Process" is of "Co-digestion". A considerable increase in the "Process Parameters" driver is observed with time. The main residues used in co-digestion are nitrogen-rich, such as algae, sewage sludge, food waste, and animal waste. In addition to contributing to the nutritional proportion of the raw material, these residues are properly disposed of and potentially increase the concentration of methane in the biogas.

The most studied process parameters over time were nitrogen concentration, carbon: nitrogen ratio, reactor temperature and raw material moisture. In the Long Term, it was possible to observe greater concern with more specific parameters, such as the characterization of the microorganisms present in the process, the initial pH and the organic load rate of the reactor.

The mesophilic and thermophilic temperature processes are comparable in the short and Medium Term; however, the mesophilic one presented a greater number of Long Term documents. The same can be said for the moisture of the raw material, comparable in the short and medium-term, but showing a greater tendency to the solid anaerobic digestion process (percentage of total solids greater than

20%) than the liquid. In this way, there would be less water waste in the Long Term and therefore less bulky will be the digestate generated for the same load of raw material inserted in the process.

The main "Multiple Stages" mentioned referred to two consecutive reactors that varied the process temperature and the moisture of the raw material, mainly.

It was not possible to identify any predominant trend of the "Post-Treatment" taxonomy over the periods analyzed. In the short and medium-term, processes for desulphurization of biogas and composting and granulation of digestate were the most mentioned.

The "Product" is a trend that stabilizes over time. It is possible to observe a reduced trend towards the production of "Bioenergy", both thermal and electrical, with time and an increase in "Other Bioproducts", with greater benefit. "Fertilizer" proved to be an important driver in the first temporal cuts.

The "Other Biofuels" driver is most mentioned in the Medium Term, mainly for the generation of biomethane and 2G ethanol. In the Short Term, few documents mention the production of biohydrogen and 2G ethanol. In the Long Term, only one document cites this taxonomy, specifically to produce dense biomass fuel.

Among the "Other Bioproducts", the animal feed was the most mentioned throughout the temporal stages. In the Short Term, the production of activated carbon is addressed in two documents.

A reduced number of players approaching the "Process Inputs" over time was observed. In the Current stage, there are companies that focus on building reactors to produce biogas and on building engines that run on biogas or lubricants for this input. In the short and Medium Term, there is a wide variety of inputs for the process, ranging from pre-treatment and reactor feed tanks to biogas storage tanks and heating systems.

Special reactors are also specified for the anaerobic digestion of raw materials with low humidity, with special homogenization systems, mainly continuous ones. In the Short Term, there is mention of semi-continuous reactors, while the Medium Term tends more towards batch reactors. The only document citing this long-term driver focuses on the design and application of a batch-style garage-type reactor.

As for the Meso "raw material" taxonomy, there is greater relevance over time, with a focus on "Wheat Straw". Over time, there is a significant increase in "Corn Straw", "Rice Straw" and "Other Straws".

3.4 Final considerations

The main benefit observed in the elaboration of this Roadmap is the possibility of more consistent planning from the players, thus allocating resources in an optimized way and increasing the organization's competitive advantage. Several considerations can be extracted from this study, whether from the point of view of the player acting alone or in partnership. From a strategic point of view, the best compositions for a company's investments or public policies are those based on partnerships and clusters of the same nature, enabling a closer relationship with the process drivers, thus ensuring the link between technology and strategy.

Based on the strategic analysis of this Roadmap, it was possible to visualize several technological and market trends. Even in the Long Term, pre-treatment was identified as the main barrier in the anaerobic digestion process from straw, being a crucial factor for solutions with less costly biological processes, such as composting and bioaddition.

It is interesting to note that the specification of the types of straw increases over time along with pretreatments. This is aligned with expectations, as different straws are composed of different cellulose, hemicellulose, and lignin. The type of raw material used allows the choice of a more specific pretreatment, which releases more bioavailable nutrients for the microorganisms present in anaerobic digestion.

The most observed types of straw were corn, rice, and wheat, which are very abundant, mainly in Chinese territory. The main process parameters, such as humidity, temperature, and pH, also require studies according to the selected raw material, but a trend towards the use of batch reactors and a dry mesophilic process in the Long Term was observed.

A great diversity of agents involved in the evolution of new technologies, together with large companies, research institutes and universities, acting in partnerships or individually to achieve their goals was observed. Verbio AG solves problems related to the supply of raw material and disposal of its solid waste by investing in local supply chains and, in exchange, providing the digestate generated as fertilizer to the landowners. This can be an interesting solution for players who want to work with the anaerobic digestion of solid waste.

Texaco is an example of a company that acted in partnership to acquire expertise on the subject. Specialized in the oil & gas sector, it currently sells special lubricating oil for industrial engines that work with biogas. The collaboration with Georgia Tech Research Corporation allowed a patent deposit that addresses a methodology to evaluate the straw crystallization index, predicting its susceptibility to enzymatic hydrolysis in association with chemical and/or physical pre-treatment to generate biogas.

The most active companies identified through the Roadmap have a main activity other than biogas production, but their expertise might contribute to some stage of the process. This fact can show a strategic positioning of the company's differentiation in line with the R&D effort in search of innovations.

Novozymes is a company specialized in the production of enzymes and has four patent documents that focus on its expertise, demonstrating its efforts for an ideal enzymatic pretreatment of the straw that makes biogas production more efficient. Shell is an oil company that currently sells lubricants for biogas engines and has a biogas clean-up plant. Its patent fits the circular economy concept by using the hydrogen sulfide extracted during the biogas upgrade process as an input in the chemical pretreatment of straw.

Among the players, the Chinese Academy of Sciences was the largest developer of R&D activities related to the theme throughout all temporal stages, presenting itself as a major driver of innovation in Chinese territory. The Roadmap analysis showed that the vast majority of documents analyzed are of Chinese origin and deposited at the State Intellectual Property Office of the P.R.C. (Sipo). It is important to highlight that most players filed their patents only in Chinese territory, indicating that there was no interest in protecting their technologies around the world. This Chinese phenomenon of large-volume production and filing of patents only in its territory without commercial purpose or pretension had been raised by The Economist (2014) and could be confirmed in this work.

Straw lacks proper disposal and can be valued through anaerobic digestion. This would enable the generation of a huge range of biofuels and bioproducts from waste that would otherwise potentially contribute to effluent, soil and air pollution. The availability of low-cost raw materials, the investments in international R&D raised in this work and the trends pointed out by the Roadmap analysis show a window of opportunity for players in the biogas production sector.

The generation of electricity from biogas, as well as the tropicalization of plants, technologies, and successful business models, reproduced from model countries can be highlighted as many of the outstanding opportunities for the development of biogas production systems from straw in Brazil.

This work allowed to observe of the behavior of the drivers of this technology over time, as well as the main national and international players involved in different temporal terms. It also allowed the identification of windows of opportunity and a glimpse of possible partners, potentially contributing to the direction of future projects in this area by national decision-makers.

REFERENCES

ANGENENT, L. T. *et al.* Production of bioenergy and biochemicals from industrial and agricultural wastewater. **Trends in Biotechnology**, v. 22, n. 9, p. 477-85, 2004.

ANTUNES, J. F. G.; AZANIA, C. A. M.; AZANIA, A. A. P. M. Impactos ambientais das queimadas de cana de açúcar. 2013. Available on: http://www.grupocultivar.com.br/ativemanager/uploads/arquivos/artigos/27-01_gc_cana.pdf. Accessed in: jan. 2017.

AUGENBRAUN, H.; MATTHEUS, E.; SARMA, D. **The Global Methane Cycle**. Education: Global Methane Inventory. National Aeronautics and Space Administration, Goddard Institute for Space Studies. ASA-GISS-ICP. Available on: https://icp.giss.nasa.gov/education/methane/intro/cycle. html. Accessed in: jan. 2017.

AVFALL SVERIGE. **Biogas from lignocellulosic biomass**. Available on: http://www.avfallsverige.se/fileadmin/uploads/Rapporter/U2012-07. pdf. Accessed in: jan. 2017.

BIOFUELS DIGEST. **BNDES approves \$23 million for sugarcane-based biogas project**. 2020. Available on: https://www.biofuelsdigest.com/ bdigest/2020/01/14/bndes-approves-23-million-for-sugarcane-based--biogas-project/. Accessed in: jan. 2021.

BIOFUELS DIGEST. **Praj to supply HPCL's compressed biogas Project**. 2021. Available on: https://www.biofuelsdigest.com/bdigest/2021/03/09/ praj-to-supply-hpcls-compressed-biogas-project/. Accessed in: mar. 2021.

BRASIL UN. **Especialistas apresentam oportunidades de negócios no setor de biogás**. 2021. Available on: https://brasil.un.org/pt-br/124933-especialistas-apresentam-oportunidades-de-negocios-no-setor-de-biogas. Accessed in: may 2021.

CIBIOGAS. **CIBiogas Energias Renováveis**. 2021. Available on: https:// cibiogas.org/quem-somos/. Accessed in: may 2021.

FAOSTAT. **Countries by commodity**. 2021. Available on: http://www.fao. org/faostat/en/#rankings/countries_by_commodity. Acessed in: mar. 2020.

FERREIRA-LEITÃO, V.; GOTTCHALK, L. M. F.; FERRADA, M. A.; NEPOMUCENO, A. L.; MOLINARI, H. B. C.; BON, E. O. P. S. **Waste Biomass Valor**, v. 1, p. 65-76, 2010.

FOODY, B.; TOLAN, J. S., inventors. Iogen Corporation, assignee. **Lignocellulosic Conversion Process Comprising Sulfur Dioxide And/ Or Sulfurous Acid Pretreatment**. Canadian patent WO2016145528A1. 22/09/2016.

FUESS, L. T.; GARCIA, M. L. Bioenergy from stillage anaerobic digestion to enhance the energy balance ratio of ethanol production. **Journal of environmental management**, v. 162, p. 102-114, 2015.

GONÇALVES, F. A. *et al*. Bioethanol production from coconuts and cactus pretreated by autohydrolysis. **Industrial Crops and Products**, Natal, v. 77, p. 1-12, 2015.

GEF BIOGAS. **GEF Biogás Brasil, Sobre o projeto**. 2021. Available on: https://www.gefbiogas.org.br/sobreoprojeto.html. Accessed in: may 2021.

GUO, R.; YANG, Z.; DAI, M.; XU, X.; LUO, S.; QINGDAO INSTITUTE OF BIOENERGY AND BIOPROCESS TECHNOLOGY, CHINESE ACADEMY OF SCIENCES, assignee. **Mechanical and hydraulic combined stirring straw anaerobic fermentation biogas preparation engineering device**. China patent CN103374521B. 26/11/2014.

JIAO, Y.; LI, G.; DING, P.; LI, P.; GAO, Z.; GUAN, S.; LI, W., inventors. HENAN AGRICULTURAL UNIVERSITY, assignee. **Crop straw co-fermentation device**. CN103436435B. 20/08/2014.

JIAO, Y.; LI, G.; DING, P.; LI, P.; GAO, Z.; GUAN, S.; LI, W., inventors. HENAN AGRICULTURAL UNIVERSITY, assignee. **Crop straw pre--treatment reaction tank**. CN103436434B. 05/11/2014.

JUTTEL, L. P. **Uso da palha de cana na produção de bioenergia**. Laboratório Nacional de Ciência e Tecnologia do Bioetanol (CTBE), 1 ago. 2011. Available on: http://cnpem.br/uso-da-palha-de-cana-na-producao-de-bioenergia/. Accessed in: jan. 2017.

KIM, J. *et al*. Effects of various pretreatments for enhanced anaerobic digestion with waste activated sludge. **Journal of Bioscience and Bioengineering**, v. 95, n. 3, p. 271-275, 2003.

LALAK, J. *et al.* Effect of biological pretreatment of Agropyron elongatum 'BAMAR' on biogas production by anaerobic digestion. **Bioresource Technology**, Lublin, v. 200, p. 194-200, 2016.

LANSING, S. *et al.* Waste treatment and biogas quality in small-scale agricultural digesters. **Bioresource Technology**, v. 99, p. 5881-5890, 2008.

LASTELLA, G. *et al.* Anaerobic digestion of semi-solid organic waste: biogas production and its purification. **Energy Conversion Management**, v. 43, n. 1, p. 63-75, 2002.

LI, Y.; JIN, Y. Effects of thermal pretreatment on acidification phase during two-phase batch anaerobic digestion of kitchen waste. **Renewable Energy**, v. 77, p. 550-557, 2015.

LUO, G.; LI, J.; HE, H.; CHEN, H., inventors. HEILONGJIANG LONG-NENG WEIYE ENVIRONMENT TECHNOLOGY CO., LTD, assignee. **Combined methane stirring device**. Patent China CN105802839A. 20/05/2016.

LUO, L.; DING, Q.; GONG, W.; WANG, Z.; LI, W.; QIN, L. Urea ammoniated pretreatment improving dry anaerobic fermentation characteristics of rice straw. **Nongye Gongcheng Xuebao/Transactions of the Chinese Society of Agricultural Engineering**, v. 31, i. 19, p. 234-239, 2015.

LYU, X.; XU, W.; WANG, X.; LIU, L.; GAO, L.; ZHANG, G.; ZHANG; X., inventors. Northwest A&F University, assignee. **Closed-loop circulating production method for co-production of straw ethanol and methane**. China patent CN105087660A, 10/11/2015.

MATA-ALVAREZ, J.; DOSTA, J.; MACÉ, S.; ASTALS, S. Codigestion of solid wastes: a review of its uses and perspectives including modeling. **Journal of Environmental Management**, v. 92, p. 1091-1096, 2011.

MATA-ALVAREZ, J.; DOSTA, J.; ROMERO-GUIZA, M.S.; FONOLL, X.; PECES, M.; ASTALS, S. A critical review on anaerobic co-digestion achievements between 2010 and 2013. **Renewable and Sustainable Energy Reviews**, v. 36, p. 412-427, 2014.

MELENDEZ, J.; LEBEL, L.; STUART, P.R. A Literature Review of Biomass Feedstocks for a Biorefinery. **Integrated Biorefineries**: Design, Analysis and Optimization. p. 433-460, 2013.

NUNES, R. M.; GUARDA, E. A.; SERRA, J. C. V. **Resíduos agroindustriais**: potencial de produção do etanol de segunda geração no Brasil. Tocantins: Universidade de Tocantins, 2013. Available on: http://www.liberato.com. br/sites/default/files/arquivos/Revista_SIER/v.%2014,%20n.%2022%20 (2013)/03.res%EDduos%20agroindustriais.pdf. Accessed in: jan. 2017.

PEREIRA Jr., N.; COUTO, M. A. P. G.; SANTA ANNA, L. M. M. Biomass of lignocellulosic composition for fuel ethanol production and the context of biorefinery. **In Series on Biotechnology, Ed. Amiga Digital UFRJ**, Rio de Janeiro, v. 2, p. 45, 2008.

PERSKE, G., inventor. Eltaga Licensing GMBH, cessionária. **Biogas plant fermenter feeding device, comprises a substance-receiving container, preferably to take solid organic substances including silage, separated slurry and/or straw and a downstream conveyor of substance receiving container.** German patent DE102010025727A1. 08/03/2012.

PINHEIRO, A. C.; GAIDZINSKI, R.; SOUZA, V. P. Utilização da casca de arroz como solvente alternativo para o tratamento de efluentes da Região Carbonífera Sul Catarinense. *In*: JORNADA DE INICIAÇÃO CIENTÍFICA – CETEM, 15., 2007. **Anais [...]** 2007. Available on: ww.cetem.gov.br/publicacao/serie_anais_XV_jic_2007/Alexandre_Clemente_Roberta_Gaizinskil. pdf. Accessed in: jan. 2017.

ROCHA, G. J. M. *et al*. Steam explosion pretreatment reproduction and alkaline delignification reactions performed on a pilot scale with sugarcane bagasse for bioethanol production. **Industrial Crops and Products**, v. 35, p. 274-279, 2011.

SANTOS, F. A. *et al*. Potencial da palha de cana-de-açúcar para produção de etanol. **Química Nova**, v. 35, n. 5, p. 1004-1010, 2012.

SHARMA, N. *et al*. Emerging biorefinery technologies for Indian forest industry to reduce GHG emissions. **Ecotoxicology and Environmental Safety**, Roorkee, v. 121, p.105-109, 2015.

SMITH, S. *et al.* Sustainable use of organic resources for bioenergy, food and water provision in rural Sub-Saharan Africa. **Renewable and Sustainable Energy Reviews**, Aberdeen, v. 50, p. 903-917, 2015.

WANG, Z.; ZOU, P., inventors. NANJING PINGYU ENVIRONMENTAL ENGINEERING CO., LTD, assignee. **High-efficiency straw biogas fermenting device**. China patent CN103045465A. 21/12/2012.

WU, A.; CAO, J.; ZHU, D.; QU, H.; WANG, P.; LI, R.; MA, B. Pilot experiment on biogas production of dry fermentation of wheat straw and cow dung with composting pre-treatment. **Nongye Gongcheng Xuebao/ Transactions of the Chinese Society of Agricultural Engineering**, v. 31, n. 22, p. 256-260, 2015.

XIONG, W.; RAINER, K.; LI, J., inventor. HUBEI LVXIN ECOLOGICAL TECHNOLOGY CO., LTD, assignee. **Pretreatment process of biogas fermentation system**. China patent CN105018536A. 07/07/2015.

XU, Y.; HE, R.; HU, J.; KANG, Z., inventors. NANJING UNIVERSITY OF TECHNOLOGY; NANJING GONGDA ENVIRONMENT TECHNOLOGY CO., LTD, assignee. **Technology for preparing organic fertilizer from blue algae, reed, and paddy rice straw**. China patent CN104119111A. 29/10/2014.

YANG, S.; XIAO, T.; LI, J.; DONG, C. Densified biomass fuels production from crop straw pretreated by anaerobic fermentation. **Nongye Gongcheng Xuebao/Transactions of the Chinese Society of Agricultural Engineering**, v. 29, i. 17, p. 182-187, 2013.

YUE, W.; DANG, J.; XIE, R., inventors. HARBIN DALIANG INDUSTRIAL CO., LTD, assignee. **Dry type anaerobic fermentation feeding device**. China patent CN103060178A. 27/12/2012.

ZENG, F.; ZENG, S., inventors. ZHONGSHAN CHENGMING AGRICULTURE TECHNOLOGY DEVELOPMENT CO., LTD, assignee. **Crop straw based culture medium and making method thereof**. China patent CN105613243A. 29/03/2016.

4

AUTOMATION AND INFORMATION TECHNOLOGIES APPLIED TO OCCUPATIONAL HEALTH AND SAFETY (OHS) MANAGEMENT

Aline Souza Tavares
Suzana Borschiver

4.1 Contextualization

4.1.1 Occupational Health and Safety Management (OHS)

Occupational health and safety Management is a comprehensive discipline that encompasses the social, mental, and physical well-being of workers, and aims to (BIT, 2009):

- The promotion and maintenance of high levels of physical, mental, and social well-being of workers in all activity sectors;

- The prevention of adverse effects on workers' health arising from their working conditions;

- The protection of workers in their work environments and the risks resulting from unhealthy conditions;

- The management and permanence of workers in a work environment adjusted to their physical and mental needs;

- The adaptation of work conditions to man.

To be successful, occupational health and safety measures require the collaboration and participation of both employers and workers in health and safety programs. Such engagement leads them to address issues related to occupational medicine, occupational hygiene, toxicology, education, training, safety engineering, ergonomics, and psychology, among others (BIT, 2009).

Since about 58% of the world's population spends a third of their adult life at work, the working environment becomes an important place to protect and promote health. Still, it is recognized that medical expenses and absenteeism are influenced by actions to promote health in the workplace. In this context, gains in the prevention of accidents or injuries at work gave rise to occupational health interventions (Steel *et al.*, 2018).

Lahiri *et al.* (2016) carried out a study with 210 workers who exerted physical effort in the market in Kolayem, Calcutta, in the period between 2011 and 2012. These workers, who were subjected to daily loads of 100 to 120 kg, underwent training with physical exercises to relieve pain related to work and discomfort in different parts of the body. The result showed savings of US$ 5,979, with the reduction of absenteeism, which entails a cost to the company.

In high-income countries, improving occupational health and safety is faced as one of the ten greatest public health-related achievements of the 20th century. As an example, the current strategic framework for occupational health and safety in the European Union (EU) can be emphasized, thereby highlighting three important challenges (Steel *et al.*, 2018):

- To strengthen the capacity of micro and small businesses to efficiently implement risk prevention strategies;
- Non-neglect of existing risks, thus improving the prevention of work-related illnesses;
- The aging of the European Union workforce.

In the European Union, the European Agency for Safety and Health at Work has carried out campaigns, partnerships with governments, organizations, and companies, to identify new risks and the imposition of directives and standards included in the national legislation of the Member States. Such regulations define how these risks must be assessed and, in some cases, set limit values for certain substances or agents (EU-Osha, 2021a). As an example, the framework directive (Directive 89/391/EEC), adopted in 1989, introduced the principle of risk assessment and defined its main elements: hazard identification; worker participation; introduction of appropriate measures; documentation, and periodic reassessment (EU-Osha, 2021b).

The directives determine safe workplace conditions as well as proper use of equipment, signaling, exposure to chemical, physical and biological agents, ergonomic and psychosocial risks inherent to the workload (EU-Osha, 2021c).

In the United States, three agencies established under the Occupational Safety and Health Act and created in 1970 manage OHS issues: Occupational Safety and Health Administration (Osha), National Institute for Occupational Safety and Health (Niosh), and Occupational Safety and Health Review Commission (OSHRC) (Osha, 2021a). Osha is part of the US Department of Labor and acts by setting and enforcing standards, as well as providing training, dissemination, education, and assistance (Osha, 2021b). Niosh, which is part of the Centers for Disease Control and Prevention (CDC) of the Department of Health and Human Services in the US, is responsible for conducting research and recommendations for the prevention of related accidents in the workplace (CDC, 2021). Created by the US Congress, OSHRC is an independent federal agency, not part of the Department of Labor or Osha, and acts as an administrative court to settle citation or penalty disputes that Osha issues to employers, following workplace inspections (OSHRC, 2021).

In Brazil, Worker´s Safety is ensured in Decree No. 7.602/11 of November 7, 2011, of the National Policy on Safety and Health at Work (PNSST), based on the following principles: universality (serving everyone), prevention, social dialogue, integrality (complete care), promotion, and health protection of health at the work environment (Brasil, 2011).

This Decree, among other norms, aims to reduce and manage work accidents, whose definition is provided in article 19 of Law No. 8.213/91. This Decree establishes that

> Accident at work is what occurs when performing work at service of a company or domestic employer or when carrying out the work of insured persons referred to in item VII of article 11 of this Law, thus causing bodily injury or functional disturbance that causes death or loss or reduction, permanent or temporary, of the ability to work (Brasil, 1991).

The PNSST has some responsibilities, such as formulating and proposing labor inspection guidelines, preparing and revising regulatory standards, elaborating studies and research related to problems that affect the health and safety of workers, among others. Within the scope of Management, some important obligations that are incumbent on the PNSST are to periodically provide information on shares; prepare an annual report on the activities carried out; and propose campaigns, all within the scope of Health and Safety at Work (Brasil, 2011).

According to data from the Occupational Health and Safety Digital Observatory (ODSST) obtained from 2012 to 2020, the largest group of agents causing accidents are machines and equipment, responsible for 15% of accidents, followed by chemical agents (14%) and fall of the same level, with 13% (ODSST, 2021).

It can be concluded that investment in workers' health and safety is important, given the number of cases and the variety of diseases in which workers are affected, as well as the expenses that this can generate for companies. In addition, one must also consider the profits that companies can obtain from the inclusion of programs aimed at worker's health.

Among the possible investments in occupational health and safety, information and automation technologies stand out, provided by the advent of Industry 4.0, such as Big Data, Internet of Things, Machine Learning, Automation, and Robotics, which will be discussed in the following items.

4.1.2 Industry 4.0 and OHS Management

The first three industrial revolutions were characterized by technical innovations aimed at improving production efficiency. Industry 4.0 is characterized by several elements of innovation, such as ubiquitous access to the internet communication between machines, and advanced data analysis. One of its main objectives is aimed at customer satisfaction, using production processes corresponding to their expectations and needs, presenting opportunities, and providing quality (Pilloni, 2018).

In the Industry 4.0, workers and customers became the core of decision-making processes. In this sense, health and safety at work became more relevant to ensure work-life balance, thus assuming that happier and healthier individuals are more productive (Pilloni, 2018). Industries direct their manufacturing with the so-called smart devices, whose technologies are involved in the Industry 4.0. Aspects of OHS are illustrated in Figure 13 and will be detailed in the following sub-items.

Figure 13 – Aspects of the Industry 4.0 and OHS

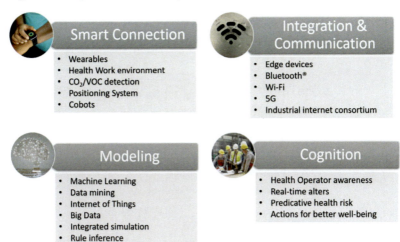

Source: own elaboration based on Badri *et al.* (2018)

4.1.2.1 Big Data

The concept of Big Data can be defined as an extensive set of data that exceeds the human capacity for intuitive analysis and conventional computing tools (Badri *et al.*, 2018). It is characterized by a constant exchange of information and data between people, devices, infrastructure, and sensors, thereby generating new data (Santos, et al, 2017). This concept has been used by companies as an important planning tool, to elaborate business models, which can predict the company's future directions. Furthermore, with Big Data, it is possible to reduce production costs (Berawi, 2018).

In occupational health and safety Management, Big Data can be used to integrate information and technologies to improve accident prevention. It offers important advantages, such as the ability to collect unlimited data, reduce uncertainty, increase the ability to analyze behavior and anticipate errors. However, like the other technologies used in the Industry 4.0, it offers some disadvantages, such as problems associated with reliability, selection criteria, and data confidentiality (Badri *et al.*, 2018).

Santos *et al.* (2017) proposed a configuration with the main components of Big Data analysis to establish a data flow from its collection to its visualization. The model is divided into seven blocks, which can be interconnected. Each block contains units that represent an important part of the overall "big data" arrangement.

- Entities/Applications: represents all big data consumers, customers, suppliers and managers, raw data consumers, indicators or metrics;

- Data Source: includes data components, dynamic libraries, files, emails, among others. Generate low or high-speed data simultaneously;

- Data Preparation: corresponds to the process of extracting data from sources to the storage layer, using a data integration platform;

- Data Storage: Refers to storing and aggregating a large volume of data in a real-time database, which is saved in a historical perspective and is later available for a limited time;

- Raw Data Editor: allows downloading of data present in the storage layer;

- Big Data Analysis: contains components that facilitate the analysis of large amounts of data;

- Security, Administration, and Monitoring: contain components that ensure the proper functioning of the entire big data structure.

Thus, Big Data can be used to identify patterns of unsafe behavior (Guo *et al.*, 2016), to monitor the presence of high-risk gases (hydrogen sulfide – H2S, carbon monoxide – CO etc.) and the quality of products in the management of the supply chain (Molka-Danielsen *et al.*, 2018), in order to direct strategies and techniques in organizations so that they can improve employee´s safety, among others. Table 2 exemplifies some Big Data applications reported in the literature to mitigate operational risks.

Table 2 – Examples of the use of Big Data by sectors

Areas	Risk mitigation examples
Manufacturing operations	Raytheon uses built-in sensors on assets to have a real-time monitoring of manufacturing assembly operations. For example, only qualified operators are allowed to carry out certain operations. To ensure quality and reduce operations risks, the sensor will also limit the number of screw turns for certain assembly operations.
Logistics	Global courier company DHL uses Big Data for early detection of potential risks (weather conditions, influenza outbreaks) in supply chains. DHL provides customers with an overview of potential disruptions of their individual supply chains.

Areas	Risk mitigation examples
Supply chain	Cisco uses Big Data to integrate risk awareness into the product and the value chain. The approach enables Cisco to anticipate emergencies by protecting important segments of the supply chain with built-in resiliency and levers to pull when a disruption occurs.
Oil & Gas	A hands-free checklist, which workers can follow while they are assembling equipment, can save time and reduce risks arising due to mistakes.

Source: adapted from Tan, Ortiz-Gallardo and Perrons (2016)

4.1.2.2 Internet of Things

K. Ashton, of the Massachusetts Institute of Technology (MIT), first proposed in 1999 the terminology Internet of Things (IoT). It is the intercommunication of objects (things) with each other and between humans, identified by a computer network. These objects are mainly what people use in the work environment, at home, at leisure, in health services, and in public life. It is estimated that by the end of 2021, more than 26 billion devices will be connected worldwide (Podgórski *et al.*, 2017).

In occupational safety management, IoT has important applicability in the development of an Occupational Safety Management System, used for the management of workers in refrigerated environments at 10°C or less, and used for transport or storage of food and pharmacist products, for example. The System is based on four modules (Tsang *et al.*, 2016):

- *Data Acquisition Module*: static and dynamic data from workers are collected. Static data, which do not require real-time updating, are age, weight, height, and cold prevention equipment. Dynamic data are, for example, the individual's position and body health statuses, such as heart rate and temperature, signal strength, and the core temperature of the environment. This data can be collected by detection equipment such as Bluetooth Low Energy (BLE) and wearable devices, forwarded to a cloud storage database, and managed in the following steps.

- *Positioning Module*: the location of workers is accurately calculated using a quick and simple approach that uses a received signal strength indicator. The inputs, therefore, are signal strength values and transceiver locations.

- *Fuzzy Logic Module*: Used to estimate time of exposure to the refrigerated environment and sufficiency of uniform insulation. To obtain this data, this step uses as a source: age, Body Mass Index (BMI), heart rate, and body temperature. After these parameters are converted from numbers to linguistic terms, they are directed to fuzzy output sets, and with pre-defined knowledge of other workers' experiences or knowledge of the facilities, they are converted back to numerical terms.

- *Cold Workplace Safety Program*: The outputs obtained from the Positioning Module and Fuzzy Logic Module stages are integrated and directed to solve problems related to occupational health in three stages: dynamic positioning, safety management, and alert management. Thus, managers can understand the situations of workers inside the facilities in real-time. In addition, warning signs can caution when individuals are in a state of danger.

4.1.2.3 *Machine Learning*

The process of using machine learning is a subfield of Artificial Intelligence. This process allows machines to think like human beings, learn and improve the execution of a specific task on their own, without human intervention (Ibrahim; Abdulazeez, 2021). The main objective of this methodology is to build a computer program that can access data and use it for learning processes. According to Ibrahim and Abdulazeez (2021) and Meng *et al.* (2020) there are many types of machine learning, among them are:

- Supervised learning: when the purpose of algorithms is to build a model from a set of already recognized input and output data;

- Unsupervised learning: when the algorithm has only input data and learns its inherent structure, extracting features and patterns on its own;

- Semi-supervised learning: it depends on both techniques (supervised and unsupervised), containing some input data already known and some not;

- Reinforcement learning: the system tries to learn through interaction with the environment. The application of these methods is used for several medical functions, such as diagnosing illnesses;

- Deep Learning: Describes techniques that simulate complex human neural systems. Compared to simple neural networks, with more layers inserted in the network confer the system has better accuracy and learning quality.

The use of intelligent machine processes has much to improve and expand, achieving adaptation to uncontrollable variables, which must be considered with the implementation of this type of process. Machines are connected in online communication, susceptible to external attacks by malicious people such as hackers (Kim *et al.*, 2018).

The scope of machine learning application in occupational health and safety is very wide. One can mention, for example, the methodology developed by Nath *et al.* (2018) to assess the levels of ergonomic risk caused by overexertion and thus prevention of musculoskeletal disorders. This was achieved by collecting movement data with time recording from smartphones assembled on the body, and automatically detecting the workers' activities, thus estimating the duration and frequency of the activity. The results indicated that when calibrated, the signals collected from an arm-mounted smartphone device could provide an accuracy of up to 90.2%.

In another approach, machine learning was used to develop leading indicators in construction projects, a way of signaling places that present a greater safety risk. This study, whose main data was obtained from a contractor in Singapore, was guided by the framework called "Cross-Industry Standard Process for Data Mining (Crisp-DM)"[1] and included safety inspection records, accident cases, and data related to the project. Five popular machine-learning algorithms were used to train models to predict the occurrence and severity of accidents, presented in Table 3. In conclusion, the prediction provided by the random forest model can be used as an indicator of the trend of security of the risk level of a website (Poh *et al.*, 2018).

Table 3 – Machine learning algorithms and their description

Algorithm	Description
Decision trees	Well known to show learned knowledge. The structure comprises a root node and an array of decision nodes ending in leaf nodes.
Random forest	A set of decision trees. This algorithm performs a ranking based on the combined results of decision trees.
Logistics regression	Branched from linear regression this linear model performs ranking rather than regression, determined by the probability of an outcome based on the values of its attributes.
k-nearest neighbors algorithm	One of the most used models in machine learning processes, whose learning is based on similarity measures that are stored.
Support vector machine	Recognized for its predictive ability among machine learning surveys in the construction industry and others. Using vector algebra, it calculates the distance between all points in the dataset and forms a hyperplane between the nearest points, thus forming a decision boundary.

Source: adapted from Poh *et al.* (2018)

---

[1] Data mining model containing 6 phases of a project's life cycle: problem understanding, data understanding, data preparation, data modeling, evaluation, and application. Through this model, the relationship between the phases is verified and cyclically revised until some desired objective is reached. Source: Kononenko and Kukar (2007).

4.1.2.4 Automation and Robotics

The application of advanced automation technology in the manufacturing process has increased considerably the automation of manufacturing processes, bringing greater quality and efficiency, as well as improving occupational health and safety (Brocal *et al.*, 2018).

As an example, in 2015, the Škoda Auto, a Volkswagen subsidiary in the Czech Republic, added the collaborative robot (Cobot) LBR IIWA 7 R800, from Kuka Robotics Corp, in its factory, to work alongside the assemblers. Several sensors placed on each of the robot's seven axes record all the workers' activities, to ensure their safety while performing the tasks (Camillo, 2016). Figure 14 below presents the main characteristics of a safe collaborative system between robot and human.

The concept employs several sensors integrated into a network. During the collaboration, robot speed and the safe distance between robot and human are monitored by a system using cameras and other sensors for real-time worker positioning. In addition, the robot's speed is reduced or a brake is likely applied if the operator moves in the area considered hazardous. Aerial cameras track human positions in real-time with the help of markers.

Figure 14 – Main characteristics of a safe collaborative system between robot and human

Source: own elaboration based on Khalid *et al.* (2018)

4.2 Methodology for technological foresight information

In this item, surveys and analyses of scientific articles and patents (granted and deposited) were carried out within the context of information and automation technologies applied to OHS management. This mapping consisted of the selection of keyword search strategies pre-selected by the Sesi Innovation Center experts. In the case of scientific articles, searches were carried out in the Scopus database[2] and, in the case of patents, the Patent Inspiration databases were used, which obtained documents from the European database Espacenet, the American USPTO, and the Brazilian INPI databases.

The keywords focused on automation and information technologies applied to the management of health and safety at work, as shown in Table 4. Several combinations were made with the terms related to the work environment (workplace OR industry OR factory OR factories OR occupational) and health and safety (health OR safety).

---

[2] Scopus database: http://www.scopus.com/. Access in: 29/09/2018.

Table 4 – Search Strategies in Prospecting for Automation and Information Technologies applied to OHS Management

Stage	Search Data Base	Document type	Keywords (Automation Technologies)	Keywords (Information Technologies)
Current Stage	ABB Technology, Intel, Siemens, McKinsey & Company, Proactive Investors, Brand Culture Company, entre outros	Reports, websites, press releases and case study research papers	("Machine Learning" OR "Deep Learning") (Automation OR Automatization)	("Information Management" OR "Analytic Management") ("Management Model" OR "Management System") ("Predictive Analysis" OR "Business Intelligence") ("Artificial Intelligence" OR AI) "Big Data" ("Internet of Things" OR IOT) "Information Technology" "Computer Vision" "Industry 4.0"
Short Term	Patent Inspiration, USPTOe INPI	Granted	("Collaborative Robotics" OR "Collaborative Robots" OR Cobots)	
Medium Term		Applications		
Long Term	Scopus	Articles and Articles in press	("Technological Solutions" OR Innovation)	

Source: own elaboration

From the results obtained, 110 scientific articles were selected, of which 34 were identified with applications in the Current Stage and 76 for the Long Term; 135 granted patents, defining the Short Term; and 120 patents filed, indicating the Medium Term.

Forty-one companies with shares or expertise in the Current Stage were identified among the websites referring to the players surveyed in the articles and patents, along with specialized media such as McKinsey & Company, Proactive Investors, among others, thus totaling 75 players.

It is noteworthy that these documents were selected after verifying their compliance with the scope of the work, excluding repetitions and patents for utility models. Searches were carried out in the titles, abstracts, keywords, and when necessary, throughout the whole document and in the case of patents, also in the claim. The period of publication of documents was restricted from 01/01/2008 to 12/31/2018.

Based on information extracted from scientific articles, selected patents, and specialized media, annual reports, company websites, and technical reports, drivers that guided technological and market trends were created (Figure 15).

Figure 15 – Taxonomies Diagram

Source: own elaboration

4.3 Technological Roadmap of "Automation and Information Technologies applied to OHS Management"

In the following items, excerpts from each temporal stage will be presented. They were prepared and analyzed according to the performance of the main players of the sector and their focus in each time horizon. The same player can be responsible for publishing the document individually or together with other players, forming partnerships. In this case, the partner´s logos will be marked by a red square. For players with documents presenting the same drivers, the logos are marked by a black square, forming a cluster of common focus.

4.3.1 Vertical Analysis: Current Stage

The Current Stage (or point zero) represents the players already involved in the development of automation and/or information technologies in the workplace through the promotion of occupational health and safety. The content of this stage was obtained from information in articles, whose understanding includes current actions, and from websites corresponding the players found in the prospective stage of scientific articles, patents granted and deposited in specialized media.

Figure 16 presents a cutout of this temporal stage of the Roadmap titled "Automation and Information Technologies applied to OHS Management". It is possible to find some clusters related to partnerships that indicate current trends in this sector, described below.

Figure 16 – Technological Roadmap – Current Stage

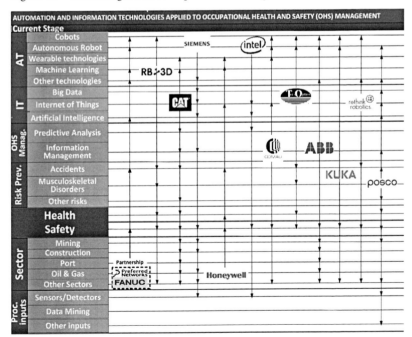

Source: own elaboration

Figure 16 shows large companies belonging to the automation and information sector, such as Caterpillar, Intel, Honeywell, Siemens, among others. Caterpillar, for example, an American company that manufactures machines, engines and heavy vehicles, works in developing "Automation Technologies" and "Process Inputs" through built-in proximity detection systems and radio frequency identification technology in protective equipment. The SmartBand Cat, for example, offers wearable personal safety, tracking employees' sleep, thus making it possible to predict risks. In addition, it performs "OHS Management" through Predictive Analysis for safety monitoring (Cat, 2021).

Fanuc Corporation, a Japanese company specialized in the manufacture of Cobots, mini robots and other products for use in factories, started to apply Artificial Intelligence functions associated with machine learning or deep learning in collaboration (Partnership 1) with the also Japanese company, Preferred Networks, Inc., focused on the development of these information technologies (Networks; Preferred, 2019).

Likewise, "Information Technologies" also exhibit similar behavior. We highlight the use of Internet of Things (IoT) associated with Big Data and Artificial Intelligence and the use of sensors and other "Process Inputs", such as software, applications and data in the cloud. Siemens, the German industrial conglomerate of digital technologies and automation, offers IoT service for healthcare and other IT services for improvement, as well as security with industrial automation solutions (Siemens, 2021).

4.3.2 Vertical Analysis: Short Term

The Short Term represents the players who have granted patents aimed at the development of "Automation and Information Technologies applied to OHS Management". Figure 17 shows the cut out of this temporal stage, where identified players claim actions that are part of the scope of this study.

The documents claimed by the inventors themselves, classified as "Individuals", were omitted from the map to maintain the visual character of this document with the logos of other players.

At this stage, the participation of large companies and multinationals such as IBM, Boeing Co., Rockwell Automation, Amazon Technologies, Microsoft Technology Licensing, among others is also observed. It was also possible to observe the filing of more than one patent granted to players such as, for example, Rockwell Automation with 17 patents, Fanuc with 8, Henan Linxiao Science and Technology Development Co. Ltd. with 6 and Boeing, IBM, and Chinese university Shandong Technology with 2 patents each.

Among Rockwell Automation's claims, we can mention a load sensor (Volts, Amperes, Watts, among others) as a "Process Input" in an energy monitoring and control system in electrical machines in the industrial environment. In addition to minimizing energy consumption and/or maintenance costs, the invention is also intended to protect the "Safety" of the worker by ensuring that failures do not occur during extreme operating conditions (US2011004426A1, 2011).

Figure 17 – Technological Roadmap – Short Term

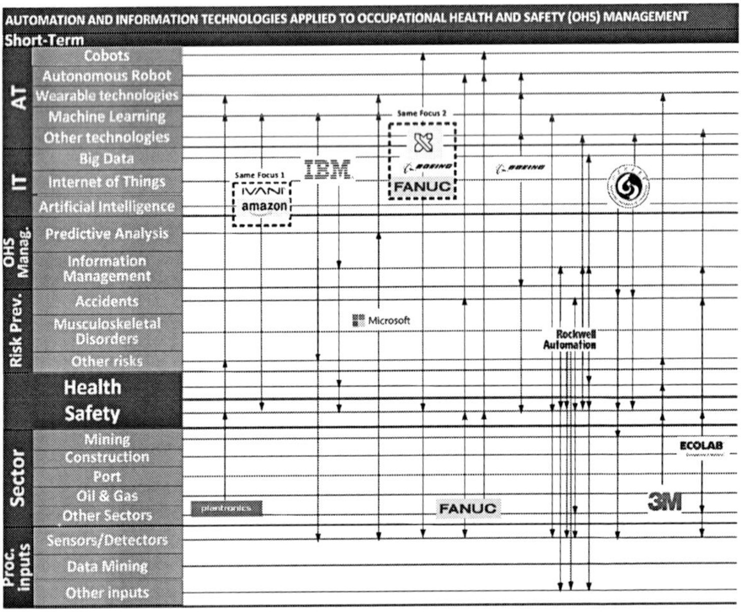

Source: own elaboration

Fanuc, a Japanese mechanical and electronic engineering company, and Boeing, an American aerospace and defense development company, for example, have the same focus related to "Automation Technology" and "Process Inputs" aimed at Occupational "Safety".

The mobile collaborative robot, which performs tasks in cooperation with one person, includes force and acceleration sensors to provide contact information between them and the environment (US2016031086A1, 2016).

4.3.3 Vertical Analysis: Medium Term

The medium term represents the players that have deposited patents aimed at the development of "Automation and Information Technologies applied to OHS Management". Figure 18 shows the cutout of this temporal stage, identifying players who claim actions that are part of the scope of the study.

As mentioned in item 4.3.2, the documents claimed by the inventors themselves were omitted from the map and classified as "Individuals" to maintain the visual character of this document showing the logos of other players.

Figure 18 – Technological Roadmap – Medium Term

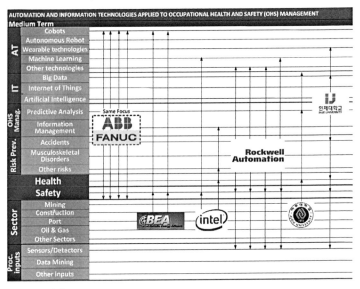

Source: own elaboration

At this stage, companies such as Rockwell Automation, Siemens, and Fanuc have participated with 4 patents each, ABB with 3 patents, and Battelle Energy Alliance, Intel, and Shenzhen Ruirongchuang Electronic Technology, with 2 patents each.

ABB is a Swiss company that offers control and automation technologies for various sectors, such as Civil Construction, Marine, Oil, and Gas, and Automotive, as well as industrial robots to improve productivity, product quality, and worker safety (CN102099614A, 2011; CN101450749A, 2009; US2008147206A1, 2018). Fanuc is a Japanese company that manufactures collaborative robots, mini robots, among other variations, for autonomous application in factories and accident prevention (US2018200881A1, 2018; CN105835029A, 2016; CN101376249A, 2009; JP2009233852A, 2009).

In the Medium Term, both have the same focus on the application of technologies aimed at occupational health and safety through different sensors in the use of Cobots and an intelligent workstation that assesses the user's comfort level.

At this stage, the foundations of cooperation between industry and Ajou University (US2016294959A1, 2016) and Inje University (WO2018147560A1, 2018), both in the Republic of Korea can be highlighted. The first company claimed a system and methodology for designing a lifestyle service that collects personal data to estimate possible user´s behaviors and steer them in a preferable direction aiming at improving their quality of life. The second company addressed a worker´s health management system and monitoring method using sensors and wearable technologies to manage safety, with technology based on biosignal.

It is important to emphasize that, as well as in the Short Term, a major presence of companies compared to universities and research centers was noted. Especially concerning cobots, the development of automation technologies was the highlight of this temporal stage for the prevention of risks associated with occupational safety.

4.3.4 Vertical Analysis: Long Term

The long-term internship represents players who published academic articles focused on the area of "Automation and Information Technologies applied to OHS Management". These articles correspond mostly to tests, studies, experiments, and research. Figure 19 shows the cut out of this temporal stage, where the players identified as part of the scope of the study are shown.

As an example, we can mention the Polytechnic University of Turin, which published a study of a parametric method for managing and evaluating the continuous occupational exposure of orchestra musicians to high sound levels. The study aimed to obtain a predictive tool to include safety in the planning of a concert season, influenced by both the rehearsal plan and the presentation to the public.

When monitoring the exposure conditions of musicians from an important European symphony orchestra, it was verified that wind instruments are the most critical in terms of levels of sound pressure (Bo *et al.*, 2016).

Figure 19 – Technological Roadmap – Long Term

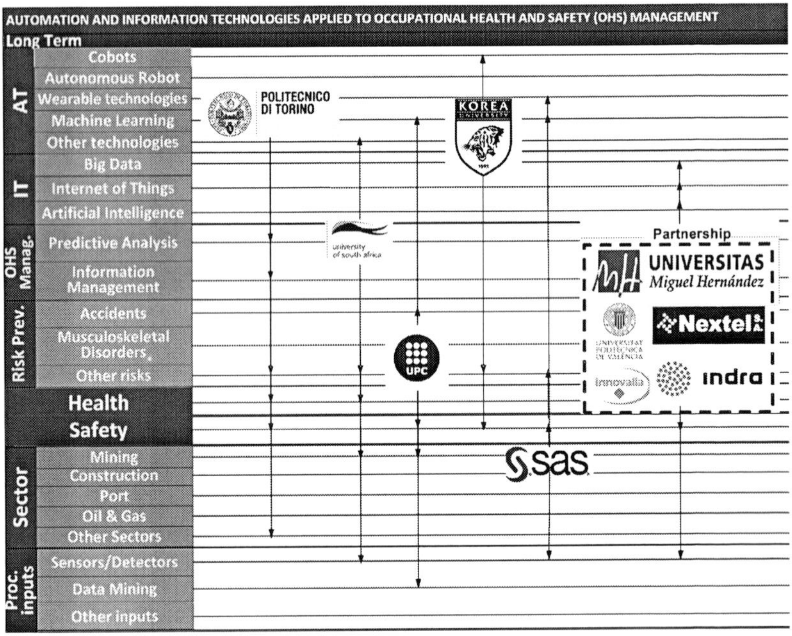

Source: own elaboration

The presence of companies such as SAS Institute, Bentley Systems, Saab Aerotech, Nextel, Indra, and Innovalia was also observed that at this temporal stage.

The universities Miguel Hernandez of Elche and Universitat Politècnica de València, in association with Nextel (Spanish telecommunications company), Indra (consultancy and technology multinational), and Innovalia (a company focused on consultancy, metrology, and technological development), created the FASyS project (Absolutely Safe and Healthy Factory), in line with the concept of European Factories of the Future (FoF). This project seeks to develop a new factory model to minimize risks to the health and safety of workers, and ensure well-being and comfort in machining, handling, and assembly of factories. A platform to monitor the status of heterogeneous wireless networks was tested, ensuring reliable and robust wireless communications needed in industrial environments to implement innovative workplace risk prevention applications (Gisbert *et al.*, 2014).

4.3.5 Horizontal and strategic Analysis

After vertical Analysis, reviews carried out according to players and their behavior in relation to drivers over time are of paramount importance. This analysis characterized as horizontal evaluates market strategies, showing their technological routes.

The first relevant analysis for a strategic understanding of the theme is the recurrence of drivers on the map along the temporal stages. The driver "Automation Technologies (AT)" can be highlighted in all temporal stages. Micro "Cobot" was one of the most mentioned both in the Current Stage and in the Medium Term. In the Short Term, there was a greater trend towards different automation technologies ("Other Technologies") and, in the Long Term, towards "Machine Learning".

Regarding "Information Technologies (IT)", fewer documents were collected that fell within the scope, in relation to (AT), that is, those that use big data, the internet of things, or artificial intelligence for security and /or occupational health. Siemens stands out for offering IoT services for healthcare and other IT services, in addition to security with industrial automation solutions (Siemens, 2021).

On the other hand, Health was a less mentioned driver in all time frames. In Short Term, for example, IBM highlighted a system to monitor the visual "Health" of a worker who frequently uses a computer to "Prevent Risks" of eyestrain. The invention includes a light meter sensor and an alert is generated to perform at least one action in response to the detection, such as "Process Inputs" (IBM, 2018).

In the Long Term, the University of Queensland, 3E Company, Shandong University of Science and Technology, The School of Mining Engineering, and Zibo Coal Mining Group Company had in common the application of an "Information Management" model focused on "Safety" of the worker in the "Mining" sector.

"Information Management" showed a virtually stable trend throughout the cutouts, including Intel, an American company strongly active in the field of information technologies, which provides predictive analytics through IoT sensors.

In the "Risk Prevention" driver, "Accident" is presented as the focus of preventive actions from Current Stage to Medium Term. In the Long Term, this trend changes to "Musculoskeletal Disorders".

As for the sectors, in general, there is a trend towards the "Construction" sector, followed by "Mining".

Another aspect to be verified in this type of analysis are the players that stand out within the subject under study. In this sense, it is worth mentioning Fanuc, a Japanese company that operates in the Current Stage with the manufacture of collaborative robots and minirobots, for autonomous application in factories and accident prevention. This company also appears in the Short Term with the filing of 8 patents granted and in the Medium Term with 4 patents filed with claims from Cobots, autonomous robots with coupled sensors, to ensure worker's safety during human-machine interaction.

Another prominent player was Rockwell Automation, a North American company that operates in the Current Stage with industrial automation, machine learning and the use of information management for various sectors, such as the Maritime Industry, Chemicals, Oil and Gas and Automotive. In addition, this company stands out in the Short Term with the filing of 17 granted patents and in the Medium Term with 4 patents filed that aim at the development of control system technologies and industrial automation in general. This technology includes sensors, and risk assessment methods in information management to promote health and safety at work.

It is worth noting the presence of research centers, such as the German Fraunhofer Institute for Computer Graphic Research IGD, which operates in the Current Stage offering consultancy, training, and analysis for the development of technologies present in the Industry 4.0, such as Big Data, cloud data management, digital assistance, sensor development, Visual Analytics, and Amplified Reality.

4.4 Final considerations

Through the examination of the Technological Roadmap and the horizontal, vertical, and player's analyses, it was possible to suggest some interesting conclusions involving the Automation and Information Technologies sector applied to Occupational Health and Safety Management.

The presence of major players operating in the sectors covered by the scope of this study can be seen, such as Caterpillar, Intel, Honeywell, IBM, ABB, and Siemens, and from different countries, which demonstrates the importance that this topic represents for the world market. The Technological Roadmap proved that the management of occupational health and safety through automation and information technologies is of interest both to companies and to research centers and universities in the most diverse periods.

The United States stood out as a country of great prominence among the technologies found, given its leadership among scientific documents, patents, and active players in the Current Stage.

It is also worth highlighting the presence of partnership clusters and of the same focus in all temporal stages with various forms propagated for the promotion of health and safety at work, thus indicating a common trend.

Both in the Current Stage and in the Short and Medium Terms, automation technologies have been the most adopted, with a focus on occupational safety and accident risk prevention. In the Long Term, there is greater attention to the development of machine learning with a view to preventing musculoskeletal disorders, occupational safety, and information management.

Among the automation technologies, we can highlight the use of collaborative robots and autonomous robots compared to other technologies. Consequently, sensors/detectors also appear of equal importance, as they assist in the sensing, detection, and emission of signals associated with these technologies.

Information technologies appeared less than the previous ones, which can be associated with its use on a larger scale with a focus on the company's information security, protection against hackers, and cyberattacks, disfavoring the issue of occupational health and safety.

As for OHS Management, there was a greater focus on the Current Stage, given the lower number of patents and research deposits for the management itself. In this context, there was a greater focus of players on Information Management models in relation to Predictive Analysis, showing similar behavior throughout the temporal stages.

It was also noticed that automation and information technologies have been applied in various sectors, highlighting Mining, Civil Construction, and Automotive, given the profile of great risks offered by their operations.

REFERENCES

BADRI, A.; BOUDREAU-TRUDEL, B.; SOUISSI, A. S. Occupational health and safety in the industry 4.0 era: A cause for major concern? **Safety Science**, v. 109, p. 403-411, 2018.

BERAWI, M. A. Utilizing big data in industry 4.0: managing competitive advantages and business ethics. **International Journal of Technology**, v. 3, p. 430-433, 2018.

BIT. Bureau Internacional do Trabalho. **Introdução à saúde e segurança no trabalho**. 2009. Disponível em: https://www.ilo.org/public/portugue/region/eurpro/lisbon/pdf/pub_modulos2.pdf. Acesso em: 2 jul. 2021.

BO, M.; CLERICO, M.; POGNANT, F. Parametric Method for the Noise Risk Assessment of Professional Orchestral Musicians. **Noise & Health**, v. 18, n. 85, 2016.

BRASIL. **Decreto nº 7.602, de 7 de novembro de 2011**. Dispõe sobre a Política Nacional de Segurança e Saúde no Trabalho – PNSST. Brasília – DF: Casa Civil, 2011.

BRASIL. **Lei nº 8.213, de 24 de julho de 1991.** Dispõe sobre os Planos de Benefícios da Previdência Social e dá outras providências. Brasília – DF: Casa Civil, 1991.

BROCAL, F.; GONZÁLEZ, C.; SEBASTIÁN, M. A. Technique to identify and characterize new and emerging risks: A new tool for application in manufacturing processes. **Safety Science,** v. 109, p. 144-156, 2018.

CAMILLO, J. Robot automatically assembles transmission with high precision. **Assembly,** v. 59, n. 2, 2016.

CAT. **CAT SMARTBAND.** Disponível em: https://www.cat.com/pt_BR/support/operations/frms/smartband.html. Acesso em: 2 jul. 2021.

CDC. **Centers for Disease Control and Prevention.** Home page. National Institute for Occupational Safety & Health (NIOSH). Disponível em: https://www.cdc.gov/index.htm. Acesso em: 18 maio 2021.

EU-OSHA. Agência Europeia para a Segurança e Saúde no Trabalho. **O que fazemos.** 2021. Disponível em: https://osha.europa.eu/pt/about-eu-osha/what-we-do. Acesso em: 18 maio 2021.

EU-OSHA. Agência Europeia para a Segurança e Saúde no Trabalho. **Directiva-quadro relativa à SST.** 2021b. Disponível em: https://osha.europa.eu/pt/legislation/directives/the-osh-framework-directive/the--osh-framework-directive-introduction. Acesso em: 18 maio 2021.

EU-OSHA. Agência Europeia para a Segurança e Saúde no trabalho. **Sondagens de opinião pan-europeias sobre segurança e saúde no trabalho.** 2021c. Disponível em: https://osha.europa.eu/pt/safety-and--health-legislation/european-directives. Acesso em: 18 maio 2021.

GISBERT, J. R. *et al.* Integrated system for control and monitoring industrial wireless networks for labor risk prevention. **Journal of Network and Computer Applications,** v. 39, n. 1, p. 233-252, 2014.

GUO, S. Y. *et al.* A Big-Data-based platform of workers' behavior: Observations from the field. **Accident Analysis and Prevention,** v. 93, p. 299-309, 2016.

IBRAHIM, I. M.; ABDULAZEEZ, A. M. The Role of Machine Learning Algorithms for Diagnosing Diseases. **Journal of Applied Science and Technology Trends**, v. 2, n. 1, p. 10-19, 2021.

KHALID, A. Security framework for industrial collaborative robotic cyber-physical systems. **Computers in Industry**, v. 97, p. 132-145, 2018.

KIM, D.-H. *et al.* Smart Machining Process Using Machine Learning: A Review and Perspective on Machining Industry. **International Journal of Precision Engineering and Manufacturing-green Technology**, v. 5, p. 555-568, 2018.

KONONENKO, I.; KUKAR, M. **Chapter 1 – Introduction, Machine Learning and Data Mining**. [S.l.]: Woodhead Publishing, 2007.

LAHIRI, S.; TEMPESTI, T.; GANGOPADHYAY, S. Is There an Economic Case for Training Intervention in the Manual Material Handling Sector of Developing Countries? **Journal of Occupational and Environmental Medicine**, v. 58, p. 329-337, 2016.

MENG, T. *et al.* A survey on machine learning for data fusion. **Information Fusion**, v. 57, p. 115-129, 2020.

MOLKA-DANIELSEN, J.; ENGELSETH, P.; WANG, H. Large scale integration of wireless sensor network technologies for air quality monitoring at a logistics shipping base. **Journal of Industrial Information Integration**, v. 10, p. 20-28, 2018.

NATH, N. D.; CHASPARI, T.; BEHZADAN, A.H. Automated ergonomic risk monitoring using body-mounted sensors and machine learning. **Advanced Engineering Informatics**, v. 38, p. 514-526, 2018.

NETWORKS, Preferred. **FANUC's new AI functions that utilize machine learning and deep learning.** 2019. Disponível em: https:// www.preferred.jp/en/news/pr20190411/. Acesso em: 2 jul. 2021.

ODSST. **Observatório Digital De Saúde E Segurança Do Trabalho.** Perfil dos Casos – CAT. Disponível em: https://smartlabbr.org/sst/localidade/0?dimensao=perfilCasosAcidentes. Acesso em: 2 jul. 2021.

OSHA. **Occupational Safety and Health Administration.** OSH Act of 1970. United States Department of Labor. Disponível em: https://www.osha.gov/laws-regs/oshact/toc. Acesso em: 18 maio 2021.

OSHA. **Occupational Safety and Health Administration.** About OSHA. United States Department of Labor. Disponível em: https://www.osha.gov/aboutosha; https://www.cdc.gov/niosh/. Acesso em: 18 maio 2021.

OSHRC. **Occupational Safety & Health Review Commission.** About the Commission. Disponível em: https://www.oshrc.gov/. Acesso em: 18 maio 2021.

PILLONI, V. How Data Will Transform Industrial Processes: Crowdsensing, Crowdsourcing and Big Data as Pillars of Industry 4.0. **Future Internet**, v. 10, p. 24, 2018.

PODGÓRSKI, D. *et al.* Towards a conceptual framework of OSH risk management in Smart Working Environments based on smart PPE, Ambient Intelligence and the Internet of Things technologies. **International Journal of Occupational Safety and Ergonomics**, v. 23, n. 1, p. 1-20, 2017.

SANTOS, M. Y. *et al.* A Big Data system supporting Bosch Braga Industry 4.0 strategy. **International Journal of Information Management**, v. 37, p. 750-760, 2017.

SIEMENS. **ABOUT US**. 2021. Disponível em: https://www.siemens-advanta.com/. Acesso em: 2 jul. 2021.

STEEL, J.; LUYTEN, J.; GODDERIS, L. **Occupational Health**: The Global Evidence and Value. ICOH2018 Congress, 2018. Disponível em: https://smartlabbr.org/sst/localidade/0?dimensao=perfilCasosAcidentes. Acesso em: set. 2022.

TAN, K. H.; ORTIZ-GALLARDO, V. G.; PERRONS, R. K. Using Big Data to manage safety-related risk in the upstream oil & gas industry: A research agenda. **Energy Exploration and Exploitation**, v. 34, n. 2, p. 282-289, 2016.

TSANG, Y. P. *et al.* An IoT-based Occupational Safety Management System in Cold Storage Facilities. **International Workshop of Advanced Manufacturing and Automation.** IWAMA 2016, 2016.

5

DIGITAL TRANSFORMATION IN OCCUPATIONAL HEALTH

Suzana Borschiver
Aline Souza Tavares
Andrezza Lemos Rangel da Silva

5.1 Contextualization

5.1.1 Macrotrends of digital transformation in health

Technologies currently occupy a significant place in the most diverse spheres of society. They range from informal to formal education, assisting in scientific research as well as in diverse work environments, thus shaping the way people communicate and even relate. Likewise, in recent years, technology has also entered the healthcare sector. Digital Authority Partners, a consultancy specialized in the implementation of digital transformation systems, published an article in 2019 presenting the synthesis of the 7 main trends for the health sector.

1. Health on demand
2. Big data in health
3. Treatment by virtual reality
4. Wearable health devices
5. Predictive health
6. Artificial intelligence (AI)
7. Electronic health records (EHR) and blockchain

The so-called "Health on Demand" is directly related to the desire of modern society concerning mobility. According to statistics presented in a 2018 article, more than 50% of all web access in the world occurred through mobile devices. Regarding the healthcare sector, consumers seek information online for the following reasons:

- 47% researching for doctors;
- 38% researching hospitals and other service points;
- 77% for appointment scheduling.

This result clearly reflects the concept of on-demand healthcare, where the availability of care is sought when and where it is needed.

Big data collects information about companies through social media, e-commerce, online transactions, and financial transactions, as well as identifies patterns and trends for future use. For the health sector, it can bring the following benefits:

- Reduction in the prescription error rate – by analyzing patient records, a software can mark any inconsistency between the patient's health and the prescribed medication, generating an alert to the doctor and the patient if any risk of error is identified.

- Facilitating preventive care – 28% of patients in hospital emergencies in the United States are recurrent. Big data analytics can generate a preventive care plan to avoid its return.

- More accurate staffing – predictive big data analytics can help hospitals and clinics estimate future admission rates, helping to allocate adequate staff to handle patients.

Regarding the trend of treatment with virtual reality, it is seen as a safe alternative to the treatment of people struggling with chronic pain which, in 2016, affected about 50 million adults in the United States. The technology is being used not only to treat pain, but also to treat anxiety, post-traumatic stress, and stroke.

Another trend is the use of wearable devices for data collection. Many patients have contact with doctors only when they are affected by an illness or only once a year. With the rise of the digital age, the focus of health will be on prevention and follow-up, generating demand for frequent health information.

As a result, healthcare companies have been proactive in investing in wearable devices that can provide up-to-date information by monitoring high-risk patients. Some of the most common devices are: Heart rate sensors, exercise trackers, sweat meters – used for diabetics to monitor blood sugar levels, Oximeters – monitor the amount of oxygen carried in the blood and is often used by patients with respiratory illnesses such as Chronic Obstructive Pulmonary Disease (COPD) or asthma.

Predictive health is another trend in this market arising with the help of big data and wearable devices. With the information aggregated through big data and other marketing sources, the collaboration with healthcare companies to develop healthy lifestyle recommendations for their patients is made possible.

As an example, it is possible to hire the analysis of the frequency of a certain word in social media channels and in the main search vehicles to determine the most common searches of medical conditions, diseases, and general health. A predictive model that anticipates where and when the next big health boom will occur can be developed and companies can prepare for that event.

On a smaller scale, predictive analytics can help companies of all sizes to hire temporary workers, as impending cold and flu outbreaks can result in a shortage of workers. Alternatively, by monitoring its employees, the companies can carry out preventive work to avoid sick leave.

Regarding the use of artificial intelligence (AI), Japanese robots, for example, act as nurses. Currently, these robots also have American versions, such as the Moxi, a friendly hospital droid designed to assist human nurses with routine tasks such as fetching and resupplying provisions.

Chatbots[3] and virtual health assistants are other AI-based technology that patients are becoming familiar with. Chatbots can play a variety of roles, from customer service representatives to diagnostic tools and even acting as therapists.

Finally, in relation to the electronic records trend, authorities and health experts have been trying to find workable solutions to the medical records issues dispersed across different platforms.

An electronic health record (EHR) is the digital version of a medical record and includes a patient's medical history and diagnosis to treatment plans, immunization dates, and test results. It also contains information such as a home address, previous workplaces, and financial information such as patients' credit card numbers. In addition, that is exactly why this information is considered sensitive and attracts the attention of hackers.

Countries like Australia and the UK have started experimenting with blockchain technology to manage medical records and transactions between patients, healthcare professionals, and insurance companies. Thanks to a decentralized network of computers that manipulate the blockchain and record simultaneously, all conflicting transactions and information are automatically detected. Records are not only 100% accurate, but they are also harder to break into.

In this context of digital transformation and technological trends, the term e-Health and its derivative, m-Health has been widely used in the literature.

e-Health refers to the use of technology (mainly including the Internet) in healthcare-related services, while m-Health includes mobile and wireless technologies (e.g. mobile apps, handheld devices) in healthcare programs. M-Health can be understood as a specific part of e-Health; therefore, we use the term e-Health as a generic term for the use of electronic or mobile devices for healthcare services.

---

[3] Chatbot is a computer program that uses increasingly improved artificial intelligence to mimic conversations with users across platforms and apps, such as on Facebook and e-commerce sites. It works as a kind of assistant that communicates and interacts with people through automated text messages.

e-Health contains 3 key elements: patient data acquisition, remote electronic data transfer, and personalized feedback from a healthcare professional.

By 2020, more than half of the member countries of the World Health Organization (WHO) had a strategy for applying e-Health. WHO has been working for the expansion of this technology, providing member states with information and guidelines for effective and standardized practice.

Similarly, the European Union holds an e-Health Network, which aims to increase the potential use of information and communication technology to improve prevention, diagnosis, treatment, monitoring, and health management.

According to the literature, this type of intervention has had a positive effect such as changing behavior in people with anxiety disorders or making cancer treatment more humane. Although some studies point out some limitations, such as the lack of randomized controlled trials, cost-effective evidence has also been promising for some specialties (e.g., teleophthalmology and telecardiology). An overview of studies related to e-Health concludes that 23% of the studies point out that e-Health generates health cost reduction and 42% bring promising evidence. However, studies of this type for occupational health are lacking.

There are currently several barriers to implementing e-Health in the sector, including skepticism among stakeholders such as nurses, doctors, nutritionists, and other professionals in the field. There is also a debate whether the introduction of e-Health into modern healthcare can influence the trust of the patient-physician relationship. Current practice shows that e-Health is more of a supplement to a substitute for other healthcare services. Its success must also be built on political, organizational, and process factors.

5.1.2 The occupational health context

Occupational health had its objectives defined in 1957 by the Joint Commission of the International Labor Organization (ILO) and World Health Organization (WHO):

> Occupational Health aims to encourage and maintain the highest level of physical and mental well-being and social protection of workers in all professions; prevent all damage caused to health by work conditions; protect against the risks resulting from the presence of agents harmful to health; place and keep the worker in a job that suits their physiological and psychological aptitudes and, in short, adapts work to man and each man to his work.

The majority of the world population spends a third of their adult life at work, responsible for positive and negative effects on workers' health. Research has shown the high rate of work-related accidents, as well as disease transmission. Additionally, there is an increasing level of stress and psychosocial risks faced daily by workers.

Like most medical specialties, Occupational Medicine faces potential threats:

- Lag in the application of emerging technologies compared to other areas.

- Increased demand for health workers around the world: The World Health Organization (WHO) Global Strategy for Human Resources in Health: Workforce 2030, published in 2016, estimated a total of 43.5 million workers in 2013 and the need for another 67.3 million in 2030. According to estimates by the Commission on Health Employment and Economic Growth of the United Nations (UN), in 2016, 40 million new health jobs would be needed in 2030.

- Global scarcity of professionals, doctors and nurses in particular: according to WHO World Health Report, there were 4.3 million health workers needed in 2006, and the corresponding projection for 2030 would be 18 million, in special doctors, and nurses.

While organizations are legally responsible for ensuring the safety and health of their employees, the current state of the working environment in industrialized countries indicates that organizations, in particular, have not been successful in this regard. Following the widespread use of digital personal health monitoring systems in private and clinical settings, organizations started to provide employees with handheld devices as part of their occupational health and safety programs.

The term Digital Occupational Health System (SSOD) is used to designate digital health monitoring systems developed for use in organizations to promote health and well-being among workers. The term Digital Occupational Health System (SSOD) is used to designate digital health monitoring systems developed for use in organizations to promote health and well-being among workers.

Although the adoption of digital personal health monitoring systems has been studied both in the private and clinical context, corporate adoption presents distinct characteristics still difficult to investigate. Sensitive and highly personal information collected added to a context outside the healthcare sector affects workers´ privacy. On the other hand, the integration between work and personal life through the introduction of SSOD can cause tension, between work and leisure or by different roles played between business and personal life. Since organizations cannot force workers to adopt the system (due to legal reasons related to the protection of personal information), in case of tensions, employees might completely reject the technology or selectively adopt it in particular cases.

A study carried out in 2017 by the University of St. Gallen in partnership with the University of Lausanne discussed that the introduction of these systems offers potential benefits not only for companies but also for workers. Although the relative advantage by companies is clear (direct effect on reducing health-related costs and absenteeism levels, indirect effect on workers´ productivity and performance), voluntary engagement by the employee is conditioned to their accordance since the company will gain control over personal health data and this may pose a threat to their privacy.

However, the relative advantages to workers are still uncertain (possibly occupational health benefits and more safety). Since for legal reasons, organizational advantages depend on voluntary adoption, it is therefore important to reduce barriers for their engagement, which in turn will be influenced by the users' mental model, actions, and organizational elements. In view of this, the study was developed to determine which factors affect the intention to use digital health systems, being conducted in two phases.

Also in relation to this study, from the point of view of designers and potential users, 4 key factors were identified as essential to be part of the systems: (1) Visibility, which is the visible availability of the users' occupational health behavior; (2) Persuasion, which is the system's ability to motivate and persuade employees to engage in healthy behavior; (3) Assistance, this being the capacity of the system to inform users and their co-workers about potential health risks or emergency situations in the surroundings; (4) Control, which refers to the users' control over their data.

It was also evident at this stage of the study that vulnerability to stress and attitude towards privacy are the personal traits that most affect the perception of the benefits when adopting the systems.

Other factors that affect this perception are related to the physical and mental pressure inherent to work. Vulnerability to stress and physical pressures affected it positively, while privacy and mental pressures affected it negatively.

A study carried out by the Mercer consultancy in 2020 showed that for American employers, these innovations would be game-changers not only providing quality and accessibility to health in the workplace but also to reduce costs, despite the resistance in using health-monitoring technologies in the organizational context. The survey, conducted in 2020, showed that 7 out of 10 employers (68%) plan to invest more in these technology solutions over the next 5 years.

Workplace health promotion (WHP) can be defined as "the combined efforts of employers, employees, and society to improve the health and well-being of people at work". The Luxembourg Declaration for Promoting Health in the Workplace, generally used as a framework for planning and executing WHP projects, has established guidelines for the success of programs:

a. All employees must be involved (participation);

b. WHP must be integrated in all important decisions and in all areas of the organization (integration);

c. All measures and programs must be oriented towards the problem-solving cycle, thus requiring analysis, priority setting, planning, implementation, continuous control, and evaluation (project management);

d. The WHP includes both individual and environmental measurements from various fields, combining risk reduction with strategies for the development of protective factors and health potentials (comprehensiveness).

e-Health tools can increase interest, motivation, and participation in WHP projects. Participation point is one of the main issues in current projects, as most project participants consist of a select group of people with healthier lifestyles. e-Health tools can support increased employee participation in projects as they can help them overcome barriers. In fact, studies have reported that e-Health tools seem to be more attractive to unhealthy employees as they offer the ability to remain anonymous.

Today, many e-Health tools are available in all areas of health promotion, including apps for sports, weight reduction, and healthy nutrition, as well as apps that address psychological factors (eg to reduce stress or fatigue, improve recovery, and coping strategies or learn new skills and abilities). Current e-Health tools focus heavily on changing individual attitudes and behaviors, and rarely on improving the working environment, such as analyzing and changing working conditions. Support for the entire WHP process (including analysis of the status, intervention development process, implementation, and other activities) is even less addressed in the e-Health tools currently developed. Therefore, solutions in this field should focus on driving the entire WHP process, especially on improving the working environment.

5.2 Methodology for technology foresight information

The initial suggestion of keywords for structuring the search was provided by the SESI experts, as indicated in Table 5.

Table 5 – Scope definition – Indication of search terms

Keywords/Indexed terms
Health 5.0 in the area of occupational health
Digital health focused on healthy and safe workplace environments
Digital health and occupational health
Digital platforms in occupational health
Communication channels on health and safety at work/health promotion
Keywords/Indexed terms
Information and communication technology in health and safety at work
Digital information on health and safety at work
Health communication technology
Behavioral change and Information and communication technology
Connected health care
Viewing health and safety information
Digital health intervention on health-related outcomes in the workplace

Source: own elaboration from Sesi

For the search for scientific articles, the tool selected was Scopus, the reference base of Elsevier Publisher, selected for its wide coverage, ease of downloading, hosting many documents, for the high relevance of scientific articles, and analyzes facilitated by the structure itself.

To perform the search, the terms must be crossed using Booleans for connection between them. The search strategies used are indicated in the list below, where the numbers in parentheses represent the number of documents obtained.

118

- "digital platforms" AND "occupational health" (3)
- "connected healthcare" (92)
- "digital health" AND "occupational health" (5)
- "communication technology" AND "occupational health" (66)
- "health 5.0" AND "occupational health" (1)
- "communication channel" AND "occupational health" (15)
- "health communication technology" (21)
- "health technology" AND "occupational health" (16)
- eHealth" AND "occupational health" (30)
- "wearable" AND "occupational health" (84)

The preliminary analysis of part of the crossings indicated that most of them referred to health risks due to the expansion of the use of technology at work and in personal life. In other cases, the volume of results was not representative for further analysis. Thus, joining the preliminary analysis with the understanding of the state of the art from the initial foresight analysis presented in the previous chapters, the following intersections were selected:

- "eHealth" AND "occupational health" (29)
- "wearable" AND "occupational health" (84)

It is worth mentioning that crossing the main keywords (eHealth and wearable) with the expression "occupational health" makes the search field more restricted and specific, ensuring more compatible results with the object of this study. By using only the main keywords, the volume of articles increases considerably.

For patent analysis, Espacenet was chosen as a search tool based on the European Patent Office, thus using the same keywords that generated results for the scientific articles. Due to the nature of the document, the expression "occupational health" was omitted, as it did not bring relevant results. The results obtained for each search were:

- *wearable devices* AND *health* (*title and abstract*) – 255 results were obtained and were chronologically ordered in descending order. The first 100 were selected for further analysis. Of these, 81 were identified as adherent to the objective of this study.

- eHealth (*title and abstract*) – 9 results were obtained.

- eHealth (*all field*) – 30 results were obtained, of which 8 were added to the previous group as they are pertinent to the purpose of this study (9 were repeated and 13 were out of scope).

Due to the low volume of results in eHealth, the documents of both searches will be analyzed in a grouped way.

5.3 Understanding technological trends from the construction and analysis of Roadmaps

Following the Neitec-UFRJ methodology, the Technological Roadmap design is built by connecting the players mapped in the foresight process with the drivers that define their areas of action in the subject under study and with the time horizon, that such action is expected to be available for the market.

To identify the similarities between the activities of the mapped players and their competitors in relation to the listed drivers, a vertical analysis was carried out and will be presented next.

5.3.1 Vertical Analysis: Current Stage

In Figure 20 it is possible to see a cutout of the map of the players acting in the "Current Stage", thus providing solutions in Digital Transformation for Occupational Health. Cluster No. 1 brings together companies with the same focus, working in "System/Software", for "Health and Safety Management", more specifically in the field of "Regulatory Documentation". All companies offer proprietary software for managing documents generated according to occupational health and safety Brazilian standards (ASO, PPP, e-Social etc.).

Player n.º **2 is the Italian Workers› Compensation Authority** (Inail) Research Area, an Italian organization whose main objectives are the reduction of accidents at work, provide insurance for workers involved in risky activities, reintegration into the labor market, as well as reintegration of victims of work accidents into social life. The analysis developed by the agency was focused on the "Type of intervention/intervention strategy", in this case, telemedicine (eHealth – Telemedicine) for the field of application "Mental health/ stress". The article "Work-related stress risk assessment in Italy: A methodological proposal adapted to regulatory guidelines" (Italy, 2013), aimed at generating a methodology for assessing the risk of stress to minimize the effects on workers.

Imtep, a player signaled by cluster nº 3, is a national company focused on occupational health management and was the first company in Brazil to carry out an occupational consultation via a telemedicine platform in April 2020. By doing so, the company was shown on the map focusing on System/software and Type/ strategy of intervention, for the field of application "Regulatory Documentation", being the technology "eHealth – Telemedicine".

The partnership shown in cluster n.º **4, is composed by the Dutch university Erasmus MC, the American Harvard, and the Staff Joint Health Care Division, of the Dutch Ministry of Defense. These players contributed with an experimental study aiming to analyze the efficiency of full remote health interventions (web-based) in the work environment and the behavior of the group when mixing remote intervention with face-to-face intervention. The article published in 2018 represented on the map shows the focus in «Effectiveness of intervention/behavior change», facing the field of application «Physical or chronic pains/dermatological diseases», through eHealth** – Generalist technology.

Figure 20 – Technological Roadmap – Current Stage

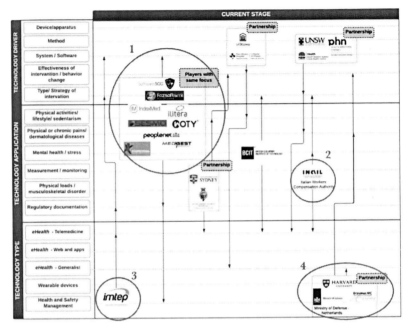

Source: own elaboration

5.3.2 Vertical Analysis: Short Term

In Figure 21 it is possible to see a cutout of the map of players acting in the "Short term". As previously indicated, this temporal stage is composed of the granted patents. It is worth highlighting the reduced volume of patents of this type, identified through the search strategy used in this study.

TECHNOLOGY ROADMAP: CASES AND OPPORTUNITIES

Figure 21 – Technological Roadmap – Short Term

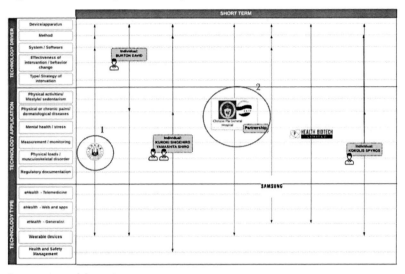

Source: own elaboration

The document marked by n.º **1, deposited by the Korean university Inha University, focuses on "Device", "Method" and "System/software" for "Wearable Device" technology. This is patent KR101866677 (B1)** – Safety management system in construction site based on wearable devices and method thereof, where the scope of protection is a safety management system at the construction site. It comprises a wearable device that mounts on a worker's body and measures health data including the worker's temperature, heart rate, blood pressure, oxygen saturation, and foot pressure using a plurality of sensors and collects worker's real-time location and altitude information.

Another example is the partnership indicated in cluster n.º **2, carried out between the Chinese Pla General hospital and the Chinese university Qingdao University, which focuses on the "Device" and the "Wearable Device" technology. The patent, issued in 2018, is CN108560250 (B)** – Preparation method of flexible strain sensor based on conductive fiber and application

123

thereof, which aims to create a method for preparing a flexible strain sensor based on conductive fiber and its application for use in wearable devices for healthcare application.

In both cases, we did not have the indication of the specific field of application for the inventions.

5.3.3 Vertical Analysis: Medium Term

In Figure 22, the cutout of the map for players operating in the "Medium term" is presented with the cutout of the identified applied patents.

Figure 22 – Technological Roadmap – Medium Term

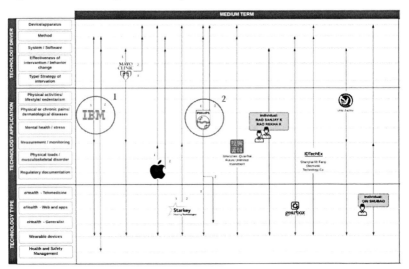

Source: own elaboration

It is possible to observe in the map the actors that stood out in the number of patent applications. An example is IBM (1), acting as a "Method" for "Measurement/Monitoring", using "Wearable Device" technology. It concerns patent US2020155078 (A1) – Health monitoring using artificial intelligence based on sensor data, filed in

2018, whose protection scope is a computer-implemented method for health monitoring using artificial intelligence based on data collected by sensors that can be attached to the body.

In addition, the company works with "Method" and "System/software" using "Wearable Device" and "OHS Management", represented by patent US2019348167 (A1) – System and method for health data management with wearable devices, filed in 2019, thus providing techniques to identify gaps in health management data and fill this gap through a subset of estimated data.

Another example is Philips (2), operating in "Device" and "Method" with "Wearable Device" technology and in "Device" for "eHealth – Generalist" technology. In the first case, it is patent US2019223787 (A1) – Method and device for health and wearable/implantable devices, filed in 2017, and protects a method for energy management of a wearable or implantable device. In the second case, US2019103189 (A1) – Augmenting eHealth interventions with learning and adaptation capabilities, from 2019, which uses a wearable device and a computer algorithm to adapt interventions to users based on the contextual information received the document.

5.3.4 Vertical Analysis: Long Term

For the Long Term, Figure 23 shows the set of partnerships represented, for example, by the Dutch university Vu University and the company Philips (1), with a study of "Effectiveness of intervention/behavior change" in the field of application "Physical activity/lifestyle/sedentarism" for "eHealth-Generalist" technology. This is the article Digital health behavior change technology: Bibliometric and scoping review of two decades of research, a bibliometric study on technologies for health behavior change.

FIGURE 23 – TECHNOLOGICAL ROADMAP – LONG TERM

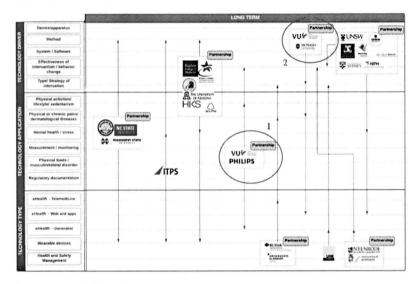

Source: own elaboration

Another example is the partnership of the same university with the Australian Monash University that works with "Type/Strategy of intervention", for the field of application of "Physical/chronic/dermatological pain" using technology " eHealth – Web and applications", through the article "Effectiveness of a multifaceted implementation strategy compared to usual care on low back pain guideline adherence among general practitioners". This is an experimental study to evaluate the effect of applying a strategy based on adherence to a guideline created in the Netherlands for the diagnosis of low back pain, without referring the patient for imaging examination.

5.3.5 Horizontal and strategic Analysis

After the vertical Analysis, it is necessary to carry out the horizontal analysis, which allows us to understand the technological trajectory over time. This analysis is important for understanding each temporal stage and the level of availability of each technology to complete the strategic reasoning about the area under study.

A first aspect to be verified in this type of analysis are the players that stand out in the subject under study. In this sense, it is worth mentioning Philips, a Dutch company with products aimed at technology, consumer products, and lifestyle, with representation in the medium and Long Term. In the Medium Term, the company acts without partnerships and is dedicated to a method of health monitoring based on artificial intelligence using sensors (wearable devices) and the construction of a computer algorithm to adapt interventions to users based on contextual information received from a wearable device. In the Long Term, the company participated in partnership with Dutch Vu University, in a bibliometric study on technologies for changing health behaviors, denoting the interest in continuing to invest in this market segment.

In the Long Term, it is worth mentioning the Dutch Vu University, one of the two large research universities financed with public funds, and which participated in two studies, thus representing a relevant partner for R&D in this segment.

Another relevant aspect for a strategic understanding of the theme is the recurrence of drivers indicated on the map. Regarding the "Focus of Action" taxonomy, it is possible to see the great representation of "Device" and "Method", which represent the players whose innovation activity is focused on the construction, application, or testing of wearable devices for health and the construction of methods of using these devices or applying interventions.

For the "Technology Application", the publications marked on the map are directed to the topic "Physical activity/lifestyle/sedentary lifestyle", in addition to "physical/chronic/dermatological diseases".

An example for the category "Physical activity/lifestyle/sedentarism" is the contribution of the partnership between the University of Ottawa and the Ottawa Hospital. In the 2018 article "The effectiveness of eHealth interventions on physical activity and measures of obesity among working-age women: a systematic review and meta-analysis" to assess the effectiveness of health technology interventions to improve physical activity levels and reduce obesity levels in working-age women (18-65 years). For the category "physical or chronic pains/dermatological diseases", the granted patent AU2018250529 (B2) – Mobile Wearable Monitoring System, issued in 2018, protects a device to determine and monitor neurological or muscle disorders.

Regarding the "Technology" driver, the emphasis is on wearable devices, which serve as an instrument for applying eHealth interventions and health monitoring in general.

Finally, it is also important to mention the characteristics of the players in this map. The contribution of individuals to the technological evolution of the subject of this study, especially in the Short Term, where 43% of players are in this category, according to the patents listed below:

- AU2018250529 (B2) – Mobile Wearable Monitoring System (Origin: Australia – deposit in 2018 – Burton David);
- JP6630980 (B2) – Health care apparatus and health care method (Origin: China – deposit in 2017 – Kuroki Shigehiro and Sanyou Soken Kk);
- US10123738 (B1) – Methods and apparatus for skin color patient monitoring (Origin: United States – deposit in 2017 – Kokolis Spyros).

5.4 Final considerations

The so-called "digital age" is a reality in modern life and is now part of several sectors of the economy, including healthcare. This digital transformation comes as a positive response to the main need of this sector, namely, accessibility and cost reduction. In this context, there is a paradigm shift in which health care starts to have a preventive character rather than the search for treatments only, after being affected by some disease.

Considering that individuals spend a large part of their lives in the workplace, the focus on preventing and improving well-being is also a demand from corporations for their employees.

Thus, health technology trends, in general, are also observed for this specific purpose. Among them is the so-called e-Health, which refers to the use of technology (mainly related to the Internet) in health-related services, in addition to wearable devices, responsible for measuring and generating data to monitor individual health conditions.

There are some important tools for mapping technological trends, such as megatrend studies, Delphi techniques, expert panels and technological horizon scanning. In the present study, a hybrid methodology was used, based on bibliometric and patentometry analysis to build a technological Roadmap.

For bibliometric analysis, the Scopus search tool was used to track scientific publications in e-Health and wearable devices for the occupational health segment; 89 relevant articles were mapped (26 in e-Health and 63 in wearable devices).

For the patentometry analysis, Espacenet was chosen as a search tool for the European Patent Office database since it contains data from more than 120 million patent documents from all over the world and brings documents filed within the scope of Wipo. The keywords used were the same that generated results for the study of scientific articles. Due to the nature of the document, the expression "occupational health" was omitted as it did not bring relevant results. A total of 98 patents were analyzed, including granted, requested and utility models.

To facilitate the understanding of technological trends in digital transformation for health, a Technological Roadmap was built based on a methodology developed by the Center for Industrial and Technological Studies at UFRJ.

From the analysis of the map, it is possible to infer that at the Current Stage, a group of companies has been dedicated to offering solutions and software with a view to complying with regulatory standards and storing the documentation generated to comply with the legislation. Regarding the players' focus, it is also possible to highlight the development and testing of wearable devices and methods and the emphasis on applications that address the worker's level of physical activity and lifestyle, in addition to the monitoring of physical and chronic diseases and dermatological.

Regarding relevant players, the Dutch company Philips stands out, with products aimed at technology, consumer products, and lifestyle, with representation in the medium and Long Term. In addition, there are technology giants such as Apple and IBM with a relevant position in the Medium Term, with 2 patents granted each. Regarding Apple, the focus is on the wearable electronic device and the composition between system and method to facilitate scientific health research using a personal wearable device with an available research mode. IBM is focused on building a computer-implemented method for health monitoring using Artificial Intelligence and a method associated with a system to identify gaps in health management data and make estimates to fill this gap.

In terms of R&D, it is worth mentioning the Dutch university Vu, which participated in two studies. One with Philips, a bibliometric study on technologies for health behavior change. Another with the Australian Monash University, an experimental study to assess the effect of applying a strategy based on adherence to a guideline created in the Netherlands for the diagnosis of low back pain, without referring the patient for imaging examination.

REFERENCES

AGAKU, I. T.; ADISA, A. O.; AYO-YUSUF, O. A.; CONNOLLY, G. N. Concern about security and privacy, and perceived control over collection and use of health information are related to withholding of health information from healthcare providers. **J Am Med Inform Assoc**, v. 21, p. 374-378, 2014.

BORSCHIVER, S.; SILVA, A. L. R. **Technology Roadmap** – Planejamento Estratégico para alinhar Mercado-Produto-Tecnologia. 2016.

BRASIL – MINISTÉRIO DA SAÚDE. **Vigitel Brasil 2019**: vigilância de fatores de risco e proteção para doenças crônicas por inquérito telefônico:

estimativas sobre frequência e distribuição sociodemográfica de fatores de risco e proteção para doenças crônicas nas capitais dos 26 estados brasileiros e no Distrito Federal em 2019; Departamento de Análise em Saúde e Vigilância de Doenças não Transmissíveis. Brasília: Ministério da Saúde, 2020.

BUCHTA, W. **Novos sistemas de assistência em saúde ocupacional**: uma resposta à escassez global de trabalhadores da saúde. Disponível em: http://www.rbmt.org.br/details/330/pt-BR/novos-sistemas-de-assistencia-em-saude-ocupacional--uma-resposta-a-escassez-global-de-trabalhadores-da-saude. Acesso em: 2 jun. 2017.

DELOITTE CENTER FOR HEALTH SOLUTIONS. **Forces of change**: The future of health The Deloitte. 2019. Disponível em: https://www2.deloitte.com/br/pt/pages/life-sciences-and-healthcare/articles/futuro-saude.html?cq_ck=1557778159962. Acesso em: 2 jun. 2017.

DELOITTE INSIGHTS. Digital health Technology – Global case studies of Health care transformation. 2019. Disponível em: https://www2.deloitte.com/us/en/insights/industry/health-care/digital-health-technology.html. Acesso em: 2 jun. 2017.

EPO – European Patent Office. **Patent Index 2019**. [S.I.], 2020. Disponível em: https://www.epo.org/about-us/annual-reports-statistics/statistics/2019.html. Acesso em: 15 out. 2020.

FRIESDORF, M.; DEETJEN, U.; SAWANT, A.; GILBERT, G.; NIEDERMANN, F. **Digital Health Ecosystems**: a payer perspective. Jul. 2019. Disponível em: https://healthcare.mckinsey.com/digital-health-ecosystems-payer-perspective/. Acesso em: 2 jun. 2017.

GIORDANO, C. S. S. **Avaliação do Technology Roadmapping (TRM) como métodos de apoio ao planejamento tecnológico**: estudo de caso do centro de tecnologia SENAI Ambiental. Rio de Janeiro, 2011.

HENNEMANN, S.; BEUTEL, M. E.; ZWERENZ, R. Ready for eHealth? Health Professionals' Acceptance and Adoption of eHealth Interventions in Inpatient Routine Care. **Journal of Health Communication**, v. 22, p. 274-284, 2017.

JIMENEZ, P.; PHIL, B. A. Ation of eHealth Tools in the Process of Workplace Health Promotion: Proposal for Design and Implementation. **J Med Internet Res**, v. 20, n. 2, e65, 2018.

MARTINS, H.; DIAS, Y. B.; CASTILHO, P.; LEITE, D. **Transformações digitais no Brasil:** insights sobre o nível de maturidade digital das empresas no país. Disponível em: https://www.mckinsey.com/br/our-insights/transformacoes-digitais-no-brasil#. Acesso em: 2 jun. 2017.

MERCER. **Health on Demand** – Global Report. Fev. 2020. Disponível em: https://www.mercer.com/our-thinking/mercer-marsh-benefits-health-on-demand.html. Acesso em: 2 jun. 2017.

NAÇÕES UNIDAS; Coronavírus mostra a necessidade de uma saúde gratuita para todas as pessoas – agora; Abr. 2020; disponível em <https://nacoesunidas.org/artigo-coronavirus-mostra-a-necessidade-de-uma-saude-gratuita-para-todas-as-pessoas-agora/>

NOGUEIRA, D. P. Incorporação da saúde ocupacional à rede primária de saúde. **Rev. Saúde Pública**, São Paulo, v. 18, n. 6, dec. 1984

PARK, S.; GARCIA, J.; COHEN, A.; VARGA, Z. **The evolution of digital healthcare**. Disponível em: https://www.nature.com/articles/d42473-019-00274-6. Acesso em: 2 jun. 2017.

REDDY, M. **Digital Transformation in Healthcare in 2020**: 7 Key Trends. Nov. 2019. Disponível em: https://www.digitalauthority.me/resources/state-of-digital-transformation-healthcare/. Acesso em: 2 jun. 2017.

SHARECARE. **Transformação digital na saúde**: o que você deve saber sobre o assunto. 2019. Disponível em: https://sharecare.com.br/noticias/transformacao-digital-na-saude/. Acesso em: 2 jun. 2017.

TAJ, F.; KLEIN, M. C. A.; VAN HALTEREN, A. Digital Health Behavior Change Technology: Bibliometric and Scoping Review of Two Decades of Research. **JMIR Mhealth Uhealth**, v. 7, i. 12, e13311, p. 1, 2019.

TRIPPE, A. **Guidelines for Preparing Patent Landscape Reports**. World Intellectual Property Organization (WIPO), 2015.

UMLAND, B. **Are employees ready for digital healthcare?** Here's what they said when we asked. Mercer Consultancy, fev. 2020. Disponível em: https://www.mercer.us/our-thinking/healthcare/are-employees-ready-for-digital-healthcare-heres-what-they-said-when-we-asked.html. Acesso em: 2 jun. 2017.

YASSAEE, M.; METTLER, T. **Digital Occupational Health Systems**: What Do Employees Think about it? Inf Syst Front, 2017.

ØYEFLATE, I.; JOHANSEN, T.; NIELSEN, C. V.; JOHNSEN, T. L.; TVEITO, T.; MOMSEN, A.-M. H. eHealth interventions to facilitate work. **JBI Evid Synth 19**, p. 2739-2759, 2021.

ABOUT THE AUTHORS

Andrezza Lemos da Silva

Chemical Engineer, graduated from the School of Chemistry at UFRJ, with a master's degree from the Program of Chemical and Biochemical Process Engineering, with a focus on Technological Management, and currently a doctoral student in the same program. Researcher at the Nucleus of Industrial and Technological Studies at UFRJ, specializing in patents as a source of technological information and technological roadmaps. My market experience includes strategic planning and improving operational and financial performance of companies.

Orcid: 0000-0002-3870-0606

Fernanda de Souza Cardoso

Chemical Engineer, Master and PhD student in Chemical and Biochemical Process Engineering at the Federal University of Rio de Janeiro (UFRJ), specialized in Management and Technological Innovation. She has experience in technological roadmaps, prospective analyses, biodiversity, waste valorization, and biogas production, as well as experience in a research laboratory of molecular biology. Nowadays, she works as a Specialist Researcher in Business Intelligence at the Instituto SENAI de Inovação em Biossintéticos e Fibras (SENAI CETIQT) in RD&I projects focused on new products and sustainable processes, based on patent analysis, market monitoring, technological prospection, and Technology Roadmaps.

Orcid: 0000-0003-1105-9107

Marcello José Pio

PhD in Management and Technological Innovation from UFRJ. Taking responsibility for the Foresight Division of the CNI National Industry Observatory. Researcher for the Defense Scenarios Group (GCD) of the LSC at the Naval War College and the CIDES

Global Network of Researchers in Panama. ILO/Cinterfor advisor on foresight methods for TVET training. Applying technological, organizational, and occupational foresight methods, as well as creating foresight scenarios in the following themes: Education, Technology and Innovation, Health, Labor Market, and Industry. Work experience in the field of foresight spans 23 years. Awarded the Brazilian Army Medal in 2021.

Orcid: 000-0003-1226-9579